Carnegie Commission on Higher Education
Sponsored Research Studies

RECENT ALUMNI AND HIGHER EDUCATION:
A SURVEY OF COLLEGE GRADUATES
Joe L. Spaeth and Andrew M. Greeley

CHANGE IN EDUCATIONAL POLICY:
SELF-STUDIES IN SELECTED COLLEGES AND
UNIVERSITIES
Dwight R. Ladd

STATE OFFICIALS AND HIGHER EDUCATION:
A SURVEY OF THE OPINIONS AND
EXPECTATIONS OF POLICY MAKERS IN NINE
STATES
Heinz Eulau and Harold Quinley

ACADEMIC DEGREE STRUCTURES:
INNOVATIVE APPROACHES
PRINCIPLES OF REFORM IN DEGREE
STRUCTURES IN THE UNITED STATES
Stephen H. Spurr

COLLEGES OF THE FORGOTTEN AMERICANS:
A PROFILE OF STATE COLLEGES AND
REGIONAL UNIVERSITIES
E. Alden Dunham

FROM BACKWATER TO MAINSTREAM:
A PROFILE OF CATHOLIC HIGHER
EDUCATION
Andrew M. Greeley

THE ECONOMICS OF THE MAJOR PRIVATE
UNIVERSITIES
William G. Bowen
(Out of print, but available from University Microfilms.)

THE FINANCE OF HIGHER EDUCATION
Howard R. Bowen
(Out of print, but available from University Microfilms.)

ALTERNATIVE METHODS OF FEDERAL
FUNDING FOR HIGHER EDUCATION
Ron Wolk

INVENTORY OF CURRENT RESEARCH ON
HIGHER EDUCATION 1968
Dale M. Heckman and Warren Bryan Martin

The following technical reports are available from the Carnegie Commission on Higher Education, 1947 Center Street, Berkeley, California 94704.

RESOURCE USE IN HIGHER EDUCATION:
TRENDS IN OUTPUT AND INPUTS, 1930–1967
June O'Neill

TRENDS AND PROJECTIONS OF PHYSICIANS
IN THE UNITED STATES 1967–2002
Mark S. Blumberg

MAY 1970:
THE CAMPUS AFTERMATH OF CAMBODIA
AND KENT STATE
Richard E. Peterson and John A. Bilorusky

The following reprints are available from the Carnegie Commission on Higher Education, 1947 Center Street, Berkeley, California 94704.

ACCELERATED PROGRAM OF MEDICAL EDUCATION, *by Mark S. Blumberg, reprinted from* JOURNAL OF MEDICAL EDUCATION, *vol. 46, no. 8, August 1971.*

SCIENTIFIC MANPOWER FOR 1970–1985, *by Allan M. Cartter, reprinted from* SCIENCE, *vol. 172, no. 3979, pp. 132–140, April 9, 1971.*

A NEW METHOD OF MEASURING STATES' HIGHER EDUCATION BURDEN, *by Neil Timm, reprinted from* THE JOURNAL OF HIGHER EDUCATION, *vol. 42, no. 1, pp. 27–33, January 1971.*

REGENT WATCHING, *by Earl F. Cheit, reprinted from* AGB REPORTS, *vol. 13, no. 6, pp. 4–13, March 1971.*

WHAT HAPPENS TO COLLEGE GENERATIONS POLITICALLY?, *by Seymour M. Lipset and Everett C. Ladd, Jr., reprinted from* THE PUBLIC INTEREST, *no. 24, Summer 1971.*

AMERICAN SOCIAL SCIENTISTS AND THE GROWTH OF CAMPUS POLITICAL ACTIVISM IN THE 1960s, *by Everett C. Ladd, Jr., and Seymour M. Lipset, reprinted from* SOCIAL SCIENCES INFORMATION, *vol. 10, no. 2, April 1971.*

THE POLITICS OF AMERICAN POLITICAL SCIENTISTS, *by Everett C. Ladd, Jr., and Seymour M. Lipset, reprinted from* PS, *vol. 4, no. 2, Spring 1971.*

THE DIVIDED PROFESSORIATE, *by Seymour M. Lipset and Everett C. Ladd, Jr., reprinted from* CHANGE, *vol. 3, no. 3, pp. 54–60, May 1971.*

JEWISH AND GENTILE ACADEMICS IN THE UNITED STATES: ACHIEVEMENTS, CULTURES AND POLITICS, *by Seymour M. Lipset and Everett C. Ladd, Jr., reprinted from* AMERICAN JEWISH YEAR BOOK, *1971.*

THE UNHOLY ALLIANCE AGAINST THE CAMPUS, *by Kenneth Keniston and Michael Lerner, reprinted from* NEW YORK TIMES MAGAZINE, *November 8, 1970 .*

PRECARIOUS PROFESSORS: NEW PATTERNS OF REPRESENTATION, *by Joseph W. Garbarino, reprinted from* INDUSTRIAL RELATIONS, *vol. 10, no. 1, February 1971.*

. . . AND WHAT PROFESSORS THINK: ABOUT STUDENT PROTEST AND MANNERS, MORALS, POLITICS, AND CHAOS ON THE CAMPUS, *by Seymour Martin Lipset and Everett Carll Ladd, Jr., reprinted from* PSYCHOLOGY TODAY, *November 1970.**

DEMAND AND SUPPLY IN U.S. HIGHER EDUCATION: A PROGRESS REPORT, *by Roy Radner and Leonard S. Miller, reprinted from* AMERICAN ECONOMIC REVIEW, *May 1970.**

RESOURCES FOR HIGHER EDUCATION: AN ECONOMIST'S VIEW, *by Theodore W. Schultz, reprinted from* JOURNAL OF POLITICAL ECONOMY, *vol. 76, no. 3, University of Chicago, May/June 1968.**

INDUSTRIAL RELATIONS AND UNIVERSITY RELATIONS, *by Clark Kerr, reprinted from* PROCEEDINGS OF THE 21ST ANNUAL WINTER MEETING OF THE INDUSTRIAL RELATIONS RESEARCH ASSOCIATION, *pp. 15–25.**

NEW CHALLENGES TO THE COLLEGE AND UNIVERSITY, *by Clark Kerr, reprinted from Kermit Gordon (ed.),* AGENDA FOR THE NATION, *The Brookings Institution, Washington, D.C., 1968.**

PRESIDENTIAL DISCONTENT, *by Clark Kerr, reprinted from David C. Nichols (ed.),* PERSPECTIVES ON CAMPUS TENSIONS: PAPERS PREPARED FOR THE SPECIAL COMMITTEE ON CAMPUS TENSIONS, *American Council on Education, Washington, D.C., September 1970.**

STUDENT PROTEST—AN INSTITUTIONAL AND NATIONAL PROFILE, by *Harold Hodgkinson*, *reprinted from* THE RECORD, *vol. 71, no. 4, May 1970.**

WHAT'S BUGGING THE STUDENTS?, by *Kenneth Keniston, reprinted from* EDUCATIONAL RECORD, *American Council on Education, Washington, D.C., Spring 1970.**

THE POLITICS OF ACADEMIA, by *Seymour Martin Lipset, reprinted from David C. Nichols* (ed.), PERSPECTIVES ON CAMPUS TENSIONS: PAPERS PREPARED FOR THE SPECIAL COMMITTEE ON CAMPUS TENSIONS, *American Council on Education, Washington, D.C., September 1970.**

*The Commission's stock of this reprint has been exhausted.

The Invisible Colleges

The Invisible Colleges

A PROFILE OF SMALL, PRIVATE COLLEGES
WITH LIMITED RESOURCES

by *Alexander W. Astin*

Director, Office of Research,
American Council on Education

and *Calvin B. T. Lee*

Chancellor, University of Maryland,
Baltimore County

with a commentary by *Ralph M. Besse*

Eighth of a Series of Profiles Sponsored by
The Carnegie Commission on Higher Education

MCGRAW-HILL BOOK COMPANY

New York   St. Louis   San Francisco   Düsseldorf
London   Sydney   Toronto   Mexico   Panama
Johannesburg   Kuala Lumpur   Montreal
New Delhi   Rio de Janeiro   Singapore

This book was set in Vladimir by University Graphics, Inc.
It was printed on acid-free, long-life paper and bound by The
Maple Press Company. The designers were Elliot Epstein and
Edward Butler. The editors were Herbert Waentig and Cheryl
Allen for McGraw-Hill Book Company and Verne A. Stadtman and
Dennis Wynn for the Carnegie Commission on Higher Education.
Alice Cohen supervised the production.

The Carnegie Commission on Higher Education,
1947 Center Street, Berkeley, California 94704,
has sponsored preparation of this profile as
part of a continuing effort to obtain and present
significant information for public discussion.
The views expressed are those of the authors.

THE INVISIBLE COLLEGES
A Profile of Small, Private Colleges with Limited Resources

Library of Congress catalog number 73-177369
123456789MAMM798765432
07-010037-3

Contents

Foreword

Almost half a million students in the United States attend private four-year colleges with relatively small enrollments and moderately selective or unselective admissions policies. These institutions constitute about one-third of all four-year colleges in the country. In size, structure, and environment, they—more than any other educational institution—probably resemble the public's impression of the "typical" American college as depicted by movies and television. But, individually, they are the least-known colleges nationally and many of them are fighting desperately for survival.

These institutions include some of the colleges described previously in other profiles prepared for the Carnegie Commission on Higher Education. They include all but two of the private colleges for Negroes that were the subject of *Between Two Worlds,* by Frank Bowles and Frank A. DeCosta. They include many of the Catholic colleges described by Andrew M. Greeley in *From Backwater to Mainstream.* They compete for students with the rapidly growing state colleges that were the subject of E. Alden Dunham's *Colleges of the Forgotten Americans.*

In their struggle for continuing existence, these colleges are likely beneficiaries of the assistance and change that have already been advocated in various reports of the Commission. For example, they need the financial assistance that would be made available through the student aid and institutional cost-of-education supplements that we recommended should be made available by the federal government in our first report, *Quality and Equality: New Levels of Federal Responsibility.* Many could benefit from the reduction of time required for students to earn the B.A. degree and from other innovations suggested in our report, *Less Time, More Options: Education Beyond the High School.* The colleges founded for Negroes, which are so heavily represented among these institutions, are the objects of recommendations in our *From Isolation to Mainstream.* In *The Invisible Colleges,* the authors recommend that colleges with less than 1,000 students increase their enrollments by "several hundred." This recommendation is consistent with a similar Commission proposal for colleges founded for Negroes. The Commission also favors state support of private institutions, which the authors consider necessary to alleviate the problems of the invisible colleges. Recommendations on that proposal are included in our report on state responsibility for postsecondary education, *The Capitol and the Campus.*

We believe that if many of the recommendations of the Commission made thus far are adopted, the problems of the "invisible" colleges will be considerably alleviated. But in this perceptive profile, Alexander W. Astin and Calvin B. T. Lee are quite correct in saying that these institutions seriously need something else — the awareness and concern of more of the public and more of the nation's educational policy makers. With this book, they have made an important and overdue beginning in meeting that need.

Clark Kerr
Chairman
The Carnegie Commission
on Higher Education

June 1971

Acknowledgments

Several other persons played key roles in the conduct of this study. Betsy Arons and Audrey Evans of Boston University assisted in many phases of the project, particularly in the preparation of materials for Chapter 2. At the American Council on Education, Gerald T. Richardson and Susan Sharp performed most of the analyses of data for Chapters 3, 4, 5, and 6, and Margo King and Barbara Blandford carried most of the burden of typing the manuscripts. The very complex and tedious job of editing the entire manuscript was performed by the expert hand of Laura Kent.

Criticisms of earlier drafts of our concluding chapter were generously supplied by John F. Morse of the American Council on Education and James T. Miller of the University of Michigan. While we were not always willing to follow their suggestions, their perceptive comments were invaluable in helping us to reshape our thinking and to tighten some of our arguments.

Finally, we should like to express our appreciation to the administrators who welcomed us so cordially on the campuses that we visited, and especially to the representatives of the 12 colleges that participated in the Danforth-sponsored conference which was held at Stevens College (Missouri) in the summer of 1969. Many of the ideas and concerns that we have attempted to present in this study are a direct outgrowth of these contacts.

1. Which Are the Invisible Colleges?

Higher education in the United States has evolved into a highly refined institutional status hierarchy that is unified by a common value system. Like most status systems, it comprises a few elite and widely known institutions, a substantial middle class, and a large number of relatively unknown and therefore "invisible" institutions. Although most Americans know the names of the prestigious private universities, the state universities, and the distinguished private colleges, and while most are aware of the expanding state colleges and the burgeoning system of two-year colleges, few realize that one of the largest segments of the higher educational population—at least one-third of all the four-year institutions—consists of relatively little-known private colleges. These colleges are worthy of study simply because of their large number; the fact that many of them may be in real danger of extinction makes a thorough examination of their problems and prospects imperative.

The Carnegie Commission on Higher Education has undertaken to study the state of higher education. A number of the studies are what we might call horizontal approaches—that is, segments of institutions of higher learning such as the Catholic colleges, the Protestant colleges, the black colleges, the state colleges, the community colleges, and the universities have been examined. This study is different insofar as it cuts across constituent lines with respect to control.

One of the first difficulties we encountered in undertaking this study was to find an appropriate title. The group of small, private institutions that concerned us is highly diverse, consisting of Roman Catholic colleges, Protestant colleges, nonsectarian colleges, black colleges, teachers colleges, and a few technological schools. Initially we thought of calling them *developing institutions,* but that appellation has come to have a number of rather narrow meanings and euphemistic overtones that are inappropriate for our purposes. Furthermore, Title III of the Higher Education Act of 1965 established a program for "strengthening developing institutions," thus making the term an operative definition for federal funding.

We finally settled on the term *invisible* for several reasons. First, it is more descriptive than evaluative. Second, it helps to focus attention on what is probably the chief problem facing such institutions: their obscurity and the consequent lack of concern for their welfare within the community of higher education. Although the problem of invisibility afflicts public as well as private institutions, we decided to exclude the public ones primarily because of the rapidly changing structure of public higher education and the nature of their financial support. We also decided to exclude two-year institutions, since many of their problems, especially those related to institutional identity (vocational versus academic emphasis, articulation with four-year colleges, and so forth) are very different from those facing four-year colleges. Finally, we decided to exclude universities from consideration, since few, if any, truly qualify as "invisible" because of their relatively large size.

PLAN OF THE STUDY In approaching our study, we felt that it would severely limit the value of our investigation if the invisible colleges were considered in isolation from the rest of higher education. Consequently, in many of the analyses, the invisible colleges are contrasted with institutions at the opposite end of the status hierarchy: the highly visible, or what we shall call the *elite,* undergraduate colleges. They are also compared with the state colleges, a group that they increasingly compete against for faculty and students, and therefore income. Finally, they are at times contrasted with the community colleges in terms of mission, student body, and other characteristics.

The remaining sections of this chapter summarize the procedures used to identify the invisible institutions and present an operational definition of institutional invisibility. In Chapter 2 the history of invisible colleges in the United States is reviewed. In Chapter 3 empirical data on the administrative characteristics of the invisible colleges are analyzed: structure, control, finances, and so forth. In Chapter 4, the characteristics of their students are described, and in Chapter 5, the characteristics of their social and intellectual climate. The impact of the invisible colleges on their students is examined in Chapter 6. In Chapter 7, we have attempted to summarize the major findings and to develop some specific policy recommendations for the future of these institutions.

Several recent studies indicate that it is possible to define the visibility of an institution in terms of only two attributes: its *selectivity,* as reflected in the average academic ability of its students, and its relative enrollment size.

The first intimation that these two institutional characteristics are particularly important came from a study (Astin, 1962) that revealed that most of the differences among institutions on 33 measures of institutional attributes could be accounted for by two general factors: size and affluence. The average academic ability of its entering students turned out to be the best single measure of an institution's affluence.

Additional support for the notion that institutional visibility is a function of size and selectivity was revealed in a recent unpublished analysis (Astin, 1970c) of data on the quality of graduate programs in different fields. Earlier, using a sample of 108 universities, Cartter (1966) had assessed the overall quality of the graduate program at each institution by means of a weighted average of the ratings given to separate departments. Departments with the lowest ratings were also those that the largest proportion of faculty declined to rate because of "insufficient information," evidence that ratings of departmental quality depend in part on departmental visibility. To determine what other institutional characteristics were related to these ratings, a regression analysis was performed, the university's overall rating being the criterion variable and some 83 measures of college characteristics being the predictor variables. As it turned out, a highly accurate estimate of the overall quality of the graduate program can be derived from two variables: size and selectivity. (It should be noted that the latter is a measure based on *undergraduates,* even though the overall quality of the *graduate* program was being assessed.) Since the weight assigned to selectivity was nearly four times as great as the weight assigned to size, it seems logical to conclude that selectivity is the more important determinant of visibility, even though size does contribute significantly to the estimate.

These earlier findings resulted in a decision to explore the feasibility of developing an objective index of institutional visibility using enrollment size and undergraduate selectivity. Information on the enrollment sizes of institutions, being a matter of public

TABLE 1   *Selectivity levels of higher educational institutions,* 1968 (N = 2,319)*

College selectivity level	Corresponding range of student mean scores		Institutions	
	SAT V + M	*ACT composite*	*Number*	*Percent*
8	1320 or higher	30 or higher	27	1.2
7	1236–1319	28–29	43	1.8
6	1154–1235	26–27	85	·3.7
5	1075–1153	25–26	141	6.1
4	998–1074	23–24	342	14.7
3	926–997	21–22	331	14.3
2	855–925	19–20	273	11.8
1	854 or lower	18 or lower	281	12.1
No estimate available	854†	19†	796	34.3

*Includes all institutions listed in the U.S. Office of Education, *Education Directory, 1967–68, Part 3: Higher Education,* 1968, except those that require prior undergraduate credits for admission.

†Estimate of the average test scores of students entering institutions in this category, based on evidence reported in Astin's *Predicting Academic Performance in College* (1971c).

SOURCE: Astin, 1971c.

record (U.S. Office of Education, 1968a), was easy to obtain, but information on selectivity was not so readily accessible. Fortunately, we were able to get direct estimates of selectivity (the mean aptitude test scores of entering freshmen) from four sources: *Amer-*

TABLE 2
Distribution of institutional selectivity by size of enrollment, 1968 (N = 2,319)

College selectivity level	Size of enrollment*			
	Less than 200	*200–499*	*500–999*	*1,000–2,499*
8	2	2	2	10
7	0	2	5	17
6	2	2	18	31
5	5	4	28	51
4	10	26	65	95
3	8	23	76	102
2	9	4	71	72
1	12	36	81	99
No estimate available	94	216	211	146
TOTAL	143	345	557	623

*Full-time equivalent.

SOURCES: U.S. Office of Education, 1968b; Astin, 1971c.

ican Universities and Colleges (Singletary, 1968), *Manual of Freshman Class Profiles* (College Entrance Examination Board, 1967), *American Junior Colleges* (Gleazer, 1967), and *Who Goes Where to College?* (Astin, 1965). Using procedures described in Astin's *Predicting Academic Performance in College* (1971c), we then converted these various estimates into a common scale.

Table 1 shows how the population of higher educational institutions was distributed with respect to selectivity in 1968. The mean test scores of entering freshman classes have been grouped into eight intervals.

In addition, there is a category that includes 854 institutions for which no direct estimate was available; independent evidence suggests that virtually all of them have very low selectivity scores (Astin, 1971c) and should be grouped in the bottom two levels.

The distribution shown in Table 1 has a marked positive skew, with the bulk of institutions scoring at the lowest levels of selectivity and only a few at the highest levels. When the "no estimate available" institutions are divided between levels one and two, the distribution takes on a "J" shape.

We next broke down the colleges in each selectivity level in terms of their enrollment size (Table 2). According to our two-dimensional scheme, the most visible institutions are those located in the upper right-hand corner of the matrix, and visibility declines as one moves toward the lower left-hand corner. As it happens, only one institu-

2,500–4,999	5,000–9,999	10,000–19,999	20,000 or more	Total
5	3	2	1	27
7	7	4	1	43
7	12	7	6	85
16	7	19	11	141
51	51	30	14	342
45	49	21	7	331
42	29	14	2	273
34	15	3	1	281
85	31	11	2	796
292	204	111	45	2,319

tion is located both at the highest selectivity level and in the largest size category, and that institution is Harvard University, an indication that the classification scheme has some validity.[1] The distribution of selectivity levels is not the same for every size category. Again, if the "no estimate available" institutions are divided up between the two lowest selectivity levels, a highly skewed distribution results for the smallest institutions, but the distribution tends to become more symmetrical as enrollment size increases. In short, the least selective institutions are highly concentrated among the small colleges, and relatively few very large institutions belong in the very low selectivity levels. Apparently, a substantial enrollment size almost guarantees a moderate degree of selectivity.

One gets a further sense of the relative importance of size and of selectivity in determining institutional visibility by comparing the institutions that have the largest enrollments with those at the highest selectivity level. Table 3 shows these two groups of institutions. Of the 27 most selective institutions, the largest (enrollments above 2,499) are almost exclusively prestigious private universities, the one exception being the University of California at San Diego. Five of the ten most selective private universities are members of the Ivy League. (The three other Ivy League institutions fall into the next highest selectivity level.) The highly selective institutions with smaller enrollments are, almost entirely, well-known private colleges. Although the highly selective institutions that have enrollments of under 500 are not widely known, it would seem that high selectivity is a sufficient condition for high visibility in all but the very smallest institutions.

Looking at the characteristics of the 45 largest institutions, one sees a very different pattern. Most of them are public rather than private universities. Also, their "eliteness" seems to fade more rapidly with declining selectivity than was the case with declining size among the selective institutions. In general, the status groupings of the large institutions conform to popular expectations. It is somewhat surprising, however, to see that such institutions as New York University, Boston University, and Syracuse University

---

[1] The designation of Harvard University's 1967–68 full-time equivalent (FTE) enrollment as "over 20,000" is taken directly from the HEGIS-II computer tape supplied to us by the U.S. Office of Education. Published data on Harvard, however, indicate that its enrollment is perhaps somewhat smaller, more like 18,000 (U.S. Office of Education, 1970). In any case, Harvard appears to have the largest FTE enrollment of any institution in the highest selectivity level.

TABLE 3 *Institutions in the highest levels of selectivity and size*

The 27 most selective institutions (level 8)	*The 45 institutions with the largest enrollments (20,000 or more)*
Enrollment = 20,000 or more	*Selectivity = 8*
Harvard University*	Harvard University
Enrollment = 10,000–19,999	*Selectivity = 7*
University of Chicago*	University of Washington
Stanford University*	*Selectivity = 6*
Enrollment = 5,000–9,999	Boston University
Brown University	City University of New York—City College‡
Massachusetts Institute of Technology*	New York University
Yale University*	Syracuse University
Enrollment = 2,500–4,999	University of California at Berkeley
Brandeis University*	University of Michigan
Dartmouth College	*Selectivity = 5*
Princeton University*	City University of New York—Brooklyn College‡
Rice University*	City University of New York—Queens College‡
University of California at San Diego*	Northeastern University
Enrollment = 1,000–2,499	Pennsylvania State University
Amherst College	Purdue University
California Institute of Technology	University of California at Los Angeles
Carleton College	University of Illinois
Pomona College	University of Minnesota
Reed College	University of Pittsburgh
Smith College	University of Texas
Swarthmore College	University of Wisconsin
Wellesley College	*Selectivity = 4*
Wesleyan University	Brigham Young University
Williams College	California State College at Long Beach‡
Enrollment = 500–999	City University of New York—Hunter College
Bryn Mawr College	Indiana University
Haverford College	Michigan State University
Enrollment = 200–499	San Francisco State College‡
Harvey Mudd College	San Jose State College‡
New College	University of Cincinnati
Enrollment less than 200	University of Florida
Deep Springs College†	University of Georgia
Webb Institute of Naval Architecture	University of Houston

TABLE 3 *(continued)*

The 27 most selective institutions (level 8)	The 45 institutions with the largest enrollments (20,000 or more)
	University of Maryland
	University of Missouri
	Wayne State University
	Selectivity = 3
	Arizona State University
	Louisiana State University
	Ohio State University
	San Diego State College‡
	Temple University
	University of Arizona
	University of Tennessee
	Selectivity = 2
	Long Beach City College†
	Long Island University‡
	Selectivity = 1
	California State College at Los Angeles‡
	Selectivity Unknown
	Miami-Dade Junior College†
	University of Puerto Rico

*University.
†Two-year college.
‡Four-year college.
NOTE: See footnote one in the text for Harvard University.

are just as selective as the Universities of Michigan and California at Berkeley and that the University of Washington is actually *more* selective than all of them. The University of California at Berkeley and the University of Michigan would probably still rank second and third in visibility among the larger institutions if the prestige of their *graduate* programs were also taken into account. It might be possible, then, to refine our definition of visibility by adding a third dimension that would reflect the prestige of the graduate departments at the institution.

With the possible exception of the junior colleges and the state colleges, most of the 45 largest institutions, even the relatively unselective ones, are visible —their existence is well known nationally. In other words, large size comes close to being a sufficient condition for visibility, although not necessarily for high status. By the same token, high selectivity may be a sufficient condition both for visibility and for status, except in the very smallest institutions.

In short, the simple classification of institutions by selectivity and size seems to provide a valid operational definition of relative institutional visibility in American higher education.

The data in Tables 2 and 3 suggest that a comparison of institutions by control and by the highest level of degree offered should reveal large differences in overall selectivity. Table 4 shows the selectivity distribution separately for each of these institutional types. As expected, the most selective category by far is the private university, where half the institutions (45.9) are in the top three selectivity levels (mean SAT Verbal plus Mathematical scores of 1154 or above). Less than 1 percent of all two-year colleges fall in the top three levels of selectivity. By contrast, the three lowest selectivity levels (mean SAT Verbal and Mathematical scores below 998 plus those whose means are unknown) include only 17 percent of the public universities and 97 percent of the public two-year colleges.

Perhaps the most heterogeneous of the six categories of institutions shown in Table 4 is the private four-year college. Of these 918 institutions — which constitute the largest of the six categories

TABLE 4 *Selectivity levels of different types of institutions, 1968 (N = 2,319)*

| College selectivity level | Percent of institutions at each level | | | | | |
| | Two-year | | Four-year | | Universities | |
	Public (N = 535)	Private (N = 247)	Public (N = 323)	Private (N = 918)	Public (N = 224)	Private (N = 72)
8	.0	.4	.0	1.8	.5	11.1
7	.2	.0	.6	3.0	.5	16.7
6	.2	.0	2.8	6.2	2.2	18.1
5	.0	1.6	2.8	10.0	12.1	12.5
4	2.1	5.7	17.6	21.9	18.3	25.0
3	7.3	7.3	22.6	18.5	12.1	5.6
2	12.5	16.6	22.3	9.5	2.7	.0
1	15.1	18.2	20.1	9.4	1.3	1.4
No estimate available	62.6	50.2	11.1	19.7	50.4	9.7

SOURCES: U.S. Office of Education, 1968*b*; Astin, 1971*c*.

TABLE 5	Selectivity level	Enrollment size			
Private four-year colleges by size and selectivity, 1968 (N = 918)		*Less than 200*	*200–499*	*500–999*	*1,000–2,499*
	8	1	2	2	10
	7	0	2	5	16
	6	2	2	16	29
	5	2	3	26	47
	4	4	16	60	89
	3	2	17	65	71
	2	2	13	40	27
	1	2	12	42	27
	Unknown	32	63	59	20
	TOTALS	47	130	315	336

SOURCES: U.S. Office of Education, 1968b; Astin, 1971c.

— more than 10 percent are in the top three selectivity levels, but at the same time more than half are in the bottom three levels.

Table 5 shows the 918 private colleges classified by size and selectivity. Well over half of these institutions (524 of 918) have selectivity scores below level 4 (combined SAT Verbal plus Mathematical scores of less than 1000). If one eliminates from this group of 524 the 30 with enrollments of 2,500 or more, the remaining 494 invisible colleges still represent more than half of all the private four-year colleges in the country, one-third of all institutions offering at least a bachelor's degree, and about 21.5 percent of all institutions of higher learning in this country. They also enroll an estimated 500,000 students, or 15 percent of all students attending four-year institutions.

At the other end of the visibility continuum, we find that there are only 44 colleges in the top two levels of selectivity (combined SAT Verbal and Mathematical scores above 1235). Although these 44 "elite" private colleges account for nearly two-thirds of all higher educational institutions on the two highest selectivity levels (see Table 1), they represent less than 5 percent of the four-year private colleges (Table 5). Many of the analyses to be reported in subsequent chapters will involve comparisons between these elite colleges and the invisible colleges.

SUMMARY If the state college and the junior college can be regarded as the second-class citizens of higher education, then the invisible college

2,500–4,999	5,000–9,999	10,000–19,999	20,000 or more	Total
1	1	0	0	17
4	0	0	0	27
5	3	0	0	57
10	3	1	0	92
21	8	3	0	201
12	3	0	0	170
4	0	0	1	87
3	0	0	0	86
4	3	0	0	181
64	21	4	1	918

is the third-class citizen, the unassimilated, the "outsider." It faces most of the same problems as the other two but always on a more severe scale. Because the invisible college is private, it gets only limited support from the state. Because it is unknown, it suffers in the competition for federal grants. Because its financial resources are pitifully scant, it cannot make attractive offers to students needing financial help. A state college, with its low tuition and government aid sources, is in a much better position to attract such students. Because the invisible college is often church-related in a society that is increasingly secular, it must grapple with the question of retaining affiliation or severing the bonds with its parent church. These are problems the public colleges never encounter.

Of all institutions of higher education, invisible colleges are the most likely to become extinct. An excellent early study in this series, E. Alden Dunham's *Colleges of the Forgotten Americans* (1969), deals with the present and future of the state college and the regional university. Many other studies have been done on the problems and promises of the community colleges, but the present study is the first to be done on a group of 494 colleges that few people know about and perhaps even fewer care about.

2. The History of the Invisible Colleges

Inasmuch as the invisible colleges, by our definition, are scattered across the entire private sector of American colleges, they differ from the most selective, prestigious, or "elite" colleges in their founding and later histories only with respect to success — or perhaps lack of success would be the better term. The invisible colleges were shaped by at least three historical forces: (a) the religious influence in America before the Civil War, (b) the demand for Negro colleges after the Civil War, and (c) the need for technical schools at the end of the nineteenth century.

Figure 1 provides a graphic presentation of the founding dates of invisible and elite colleges. Note that 18 percent of the elite colleges, but only two invisible colleges, were founded prior to 1800. By 1850, more than half of the elite colleges (56 percent), but slightly less than 10 percent of the invisible colleges, had been founded. During the next half century (1850–1899), however, a total of 212, or nearly 44 percent, of all the invisible colleges were founded, whereas the proportion of newly founded elite colleges began to dwindle.

THE RELIGIOUS INFLUENCE The history of invisible colleges in the United States can be traced back to the religious influences that were at work in America from its beginnings. With the exception of the University of Pennsylvania, all the private institutions of higher education that came into existence during the colonial period were founded by a religious denomination or sect. It was only natural that education and religion be linked, since the American model for higher education was the British university, where education was viewed as one means for serving the purposes of God (Wicke, 1964). One cannot clearly determine which priority — religious self-perpetuation or classical education — was foremost in the minds of the college

FIGURE 1: *Founding dates of invisible and elite colleges*

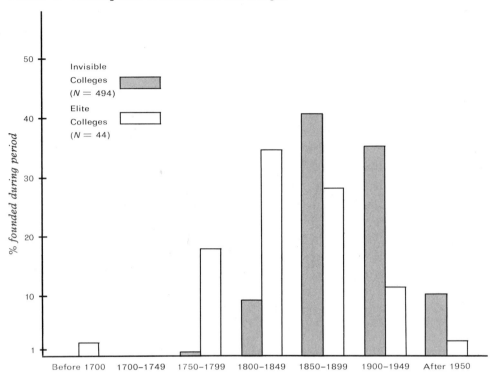

founders. Brubacher and Rudy state that "it is useless to argue whether the colonial colleges were intended to be theological seminaries or schools of higher culture for laymen. They were clearly designed for both functions" (1958, p. 6).

The powerful Protestant influence in colonial America provided the strength, the means, and the motivation for the founding of hundreds of colleges, which spread the word of God to isolated areas where religion might be weak. Although the intent of church leaders to educate was certainly sincere, one may assume that their intent to proselytize was equally strong. Between 1822 and 1865, the Methodists founded 32 colleges, 13 of which appear among our 494 invisible colleges. According to Gross, "the first leaders of American Methodism no doubt believed . . . that the future of the church depended upon the education and religious instruction of the children of Methodists" (1959, p. 11). The main purpose of founding colleges was to present a program of Christian education, which meant "forming the minds of youth, through divine aid, to wisdom and holiness; by instilling into their tender minds the principle of true religion, speculative, experimental, and practical, and training them in the ancient way, that they [might] be rational scriptural Christians" (p. 16).

On the other hand, Wicke takes a somewhat broader view, attributing this proliferation of colleges to "an essentially Protestant ethic emphasizing the need for an educated ministry and laity, of the necessity for early self-government, and of the prevailing philosophic climate of the seventeenth and eighteenth centuries during the nation's founding years. . . . Its primary task was to prepare an educated population which would enter the professions of law, medicine, and theology" (1964, pp. 5–6).

In the end, however, one historian summed up this pre-Civil War period of college founding as "The Great Retrogression." Similarly, in his survey of American Catholic higher education, Hassenger bluntly states that "the characteristic institution before the Civil War was the small, church-related college that was academically inferior but took religion very seriously" (1967, p. 31).

This onslaught of college founding reflected not only the denominational need for ministers but also the fear of the churches that secularism was on the rise (Patillo & MacKenzie, 1966). The Episcopal colleges, for instance, analyze their college-founding effort as "an attempt to further the aims of the Episcopal Church, either directly through the preliminary training of future Episcopal priests, or indirectly through a missionary effort directed later at Negroes" (O'Connor, 1969). The church leaders anticipated the rise of secular institutions, and indeed their anxieties had some foundation, for the number of state-established secular institutions increased greatly later in the century. In short, church-related colleges were founded both to promote the interests of the church and to offset the potential threat of secular institutions (Brubacher & Rudy, 1958).

In the first half of the nineteenth century, neither the states nor the federal government was yet strong enough to enter the field of higher education in full force. They were content to leave such efforts to the eager churches. Judging from the colleges in our sample, the Methodists were busy founding colleges in the Southeast, while the Presbyterians were concentrating on Tennessee, Pennsylvania, and Arkansas, and later on the Dakotas, Kansas, and Missouri.

Later in the century, the Catholics and Baptists entered higher education. Within the universe of invisible colleges, the Catholics founded 29 between 1860 and 1900 and another 66 between 1900 and 1950. The Baptists founded 14 of the 494 colleges in our survey between 1865 and 1900.

The state governments, however, were not totally disinterested in the founding of private colleges. In 1819 the government of New Hampshire brought a case against Dartmouth College, insisting that the state have the major voice in running the college and, in essence, attempting to establish state control over all colleges within its borders. In a historic judgment, the courts decided that Dartmouth could maintain its "private" status without state intervention. Before the Dartmouth case came up, the churches had been concerned over the possibility of state interference, but this decision "gave new impetus to the founding of private, liberal arts colleges" (Patillo & MacKenzie, 1966, p. 5).

As the Civil War approached, efforts to establish a system of higher education tended to be isolated and dispersed rather than planned and organized. Among the colleges in our survey, for example, the states where the most energy was expended on college founding were Tennessee, with seven colleges; Kentucky and Pennsylvania, with six colleges each; Illinois and Indiana, with five colleges each; and Alabama, Maryland, and Ohio, with four colleges each. Private higher education in states such as Massachusetts, New York, and Virginia—where many colleges had been founded in the eighteenth century—changed very little during the second half of the nineteenth century. No one can be sure why some states were so active during this period and others were not. Often a concentration of the members of a particular denomination determined the location of a college; such was the case with the first Methodist college founded in Maryland, where one-third of all American Methodists lived. On the other hand, the states of Indiana, Tennessee, Kentucky, and Missouri were then considered part of the frontier. As the population grew in these states, so also did their attractiveness as locations for new colleges. Moreover, the farther away the churches could get from the Eastern colleges founded in the eighteenth and nineteenth centuries, the less severe the competition.

Jencks and Riesman relate the concept of localism to the religious efforts of the times, pointing out that "localism . . . in most instances involved sectarian, ethnic, and economic differences in viewpoint. Since the early nineteenth century was an era when there were nearly as many would-be college presidents and would-be college towns as would-be college students, new institutions exploited all these differences and potential conflicts to attract students from their too-numerous competitors" (1968, p. 314).

The location of these colleges often proved disastrous to their survival. Frequently a college was established in a remote place not by design but out of misjudgment about the promise of that region (Wicke, 1964). The Methodists said of their college-founding leader, "Asbury [had] a genius for locating schools in out-of-the-way and inaccessible places. . . . His objective for doing so was to 'shield students from temptation'" (Gross, 1959, p. 30). Even today the isolation of many of the church-related invisible colleges is evidenced by the difficulty one has in tracking them down, a task that even education associations find formidable. In some cases, it took us two weeks to discover in which state some of these smaller colleges were located. In all, fewer than 20 percent of our 494 invisible colleges are located in or near a major city, and some are hundreds of miles from any city. While an isolated college can often effectively serve the needs of an immediate area, it cannot benefit other regions of the country; the lack of transportation in the nineteenth century made this isolation a particularly severe problem. Later some college founders, grown wiser, began to build their colleges along the railway belt westward.

Competition among religious sects was common throughout the history of college founding; within our sample, 33 different religions or religious sects, spread out over 48 states, are represented. Furthermore, a religious sect often competed with itself by establishing two colleges in the same area.

It is hard to assess just how direct and severe competition among religious groups was in the early founding period, since many colleges did not survive; but it obviously existed. The locations of 30 American Baptist colleges and 22 Southern Baptist colleges in our survey clearly attest to this fact. Seventy percent of the American Baptist colleges and half the Southern Baptist colleges in our survey were founded before 1900; frequently, the Southern Baptists moved in just a few years after the American Baptists had founded a college in a particular state. The competition continued into the twentieth century. Although the American Baptists seem to have stopped founding colleges about 1946, the Southern Baptists have created five more colleges since then, two of them in Texas alone.

Over 40 percent of the colleges in our sample, including 157 of the nonsectarian institutions, were founded between 1880 and 1920. It was during the post-Civil War period that Catholic institutions became more prominent in the educational landscape. Although 41 Catholic colleges had been founded before the mid-nineteenth century (only 12 of these survive today), the subsequent massive immigration of Catholics to this country after 1850 substantially accelerated the establishment of Catholic colleges (Gleason, 1967). Of the invisible Catholic colleges, 63 percent were founded after 1900, compared with only 37 percent founded prior to that date. Before the Catholics entered the scene in full force, most of the colleges were being established by the Presbyterians and the Congregationalists, with the Methodists and Baptists close behind. But as the Catholic immigrants moved up the American social ladder, they demanded greater educational opportunities for themselves and their children. The Catholic Church, like the Protestant denominations, believed that its own colleges could best offer the students a synthesis of classical humanism, sound philosophy, and the "true" religion.

Finally, the period between 1900 and 1950 saw the rise of the "bible college," a four-year institution devoted to the training of clergy and other church workers through study of the Bible. Twenty-five bible colleges were established during these 50 years, advertising then, as now, a broad Christian spectrum called "interdenominational" in their catalogs. These 25 colleges can be classed in the invisible college category, uneasy bedfellows though they be with the invisible liberal arts colleges.

One of the striking differences between the development of the elite colleges and that of the invisible colleges is the extent to which the invisible colleges have retained their church affiliations while the elite colleges have dropped theirs. Of the 44 elite colleges in our comparison group, 43 percent were nonsectarian to begin with, but another 40 percent were founded by a religious sect and have since completely disaffiliated themselves from the church. Looking more closely at the sects that "lost" affiliation with their elite colleges, we find that the Baptists lost five institutions; the Congregationalists, four; the Christian Church, three; the Society of Friends, two; the Episcopalians, one; the Presbyterians, one; the Methodists, one; and the Church of Christ, two. Of the few elite colleges that have retained their religious affiliations to the present time, two are Roman Catholic, three are Presbyterian, one is Methodist, one is Society of Friends, and one is Protestant Episcopal. Most of the elite colleges had broken away from the parent church by the early part of the twentieth century. Other colleges currently calling themselves nonsectarian never disaffiliated themselves formally but, instead, slowly evolved to their present nonsectarian status.

While the highly selective colleges were busy dropping their religious affiliations, most of the colleges in our survey remained loyal to the church that founded them. Only 2 percent of the originally church-related invisible colleges have broken away completely. The rest gingerly handle the situation in other ways. For instance, some list themselves as "nonsectarian" in the official U.S. Office of Education's *Education Directory* and, at the same time, continue to state in their catalogs that they are religiously oriented. Another device is to change the name of the college so that it does not so clearly suggest a religious orientation. Both methods of coping with the difficulties of religious affiliation reflect the pressures of our increasingly secularized contemporary society.

Historically, the churches have played only a minor role in the economic lives of the various colleges; their primary role has been policy setting or attitudinal. In fact, the financial relationship between church and college has typically resulted in more problems — of control and influence —than benefits for the college. An invisible, church-related college must continually consider the question of whether to remain sectarian. Patillo and MacKenzie state that "somewhat less than one-half of the colleges and universities . . . receive from 1 to 25 percent of their educational and general income from official church sources, while only 5 percent receive more than one-half from those sources. One-fourth of the institutions receive no church financial support at all" (1966, p. 28). Clearly, colleges do not remain attached to their founding churches for financial reasons. Moreover, a church-related college runs the risk of receiving few, if any, federal and state funds. The democratic principle of separation between church and state makes the funding of a sectarian institution a prickly and uncomfortable matter. The temptation, then, for a sectarian college to become nonsectarian is great.

THE DEVELOPMENT OF THE PREDOMINANTLY BLACK COLLEGES Much has already been written about the history of predominantly Negro colleges. For our purposes, it is sufficient to underline several important historical points.

As early as 1846, the American Missionary Association was formed with the intention of bringing higher education to the

Negro. According to McGrath (1965), it helped establish six Negro educational institutions prior to 1860. (In addition, it organized many more, in cooperation with the Freedman's Bureau, following the Civil War.) Still, Negro higher education was virtually non-existent until after the Civil War, and even then most of the older Negro schools began their work at the elementary and secondary level and only later moved into the collegiate sphere. McGrath points out that "these institutions arose to serve a disadvantaged group in American society, and as a result, they have had to devote much time to remedial work and have had to put the emphasis of their curricula on a limited number of utilitarian and vocational ends" (1965, pp. 16–17). In short, the original purposes of pre-dominantly Negro colleges differed from those of other liberal arts colleges.

Historically, McGrath says, most of the predominantly Negro colleges are an outgrowth of three major forces:

1   The missionary work done by the American churches, for the most part those that support colleges in our sample: Disciples of Christ, American Baptist, Southern Baptist, African Methodist Episcopal, Christian Methodist Episcopal, Presbyterian, Roman Catholic, Protestant Episcopal, and Seventh-Day Adventist

2   The land-grant legislation acts

3   The development of normal schools (1965, p. 11)

Today all but two, Lincoln University (Missouri) and Hampton Institute (Virginia), of the predominantly black private four-year colleges fall within our operational definition of *invisible* and con-stitute 8.9 percent of our sample.

THE DEVELOP-MENT OF VOCATIONAL TRAINING SCHOOLS   During the post-Civil War era, the church-affiliated liberal arts colleges began to be faced by serious competition from a new type of institution. In the face of a rapidly developing technology, many people felt that the small liberal arts college could not fulfill the function of training its students to fill specific industrial needs. Hence the technical college came into being in the second part of the nineteenth century, although not until the Morrill Act of 1862 did it receive encouragement and financial support from the federal government. Within the universe of the invisible colleges, 30 per-cent of these nonsectarian, vocationally oriented schools were established between 1862 and 1900. But the real surge took place between 1900 and 1970, when 70 percent of the nonsectarian institutions in our survey were founded. The overwhelming majority had programs geared toward professional training in industrial technology, the fine arts, and elementary and secondary teaching.

The nonsectarian technical institution had as its sole purpose the training of young people for specific tasks in a specialized society: as teachers, artists, technicians, and so forth. Gleason remarks that their approaches to education separated the Catholic college from the nonsectarian college. The latter emphasized scientific and technical trends and was flexible in its approach, vocational in its aim, and democratic in its social orientation. The purpose of the former was religious; it was literary and humanistic in spirit, rigid in its approach, and elitist in its social orientation. Unlike the church-related college, the vocational college was not concerned with the student's soul or his morals (1967, p. 46).

At first, the churches did not feel particularly threatened by these schools; they were confident that they could perform the role of educator more comprehensively and successfully because they claimed to care about the "whole student." They did fear, however, that state and federal support would be forthcoming more quickly to the nonsectarian schools than to them. Gradually, the vocational college began to include in its curriculum the humanities and the social sciences and so came more and more to resemble the liberal arts college. Of the 97 schools in our survey that began as nonsectarian, none was founded as a liberal arts college. Yet today 44 of them have branched into the liberal arts while retaining their original focus on vocational training.

The success of nonsectarian institutions was largely a result of their emphasis on vocational training and the greater earning power such training gave to their graduates. At the same time, students at the liberal arts colleges, motivated by economic concerns, began to demand that their colleges offer the option of a professional degree in four years; hence, vocational curricula were gradually added. In this way, instead of remaining distinctive in their educational roles, the church-related liberal arts college and the nonsectarian vocational college have become more alike and have increasingly competed for the same students. Wiggins claims that "in the main, Southern culture measures the values of higher education to this day in terms of increased earning power and elevated social position" (1966, p. 44), and certainly this statement applies to many students throughout the United States.

Nonsectarian vocational colleges, then, were created to answer a need that the church-related college was not interested in satisfying. Because the curricular offerings of the vocational colleges were specific, and in the post-Civil War era unique, the institutions tended to compete less with each other and thus had a better chance of survival. In addition, they have suffered less from an identity crisis than have the liberal arts colleges: usually, there is a definite body of knowledge and definite set of skills that a technician must learn if he is to be competent in his field. The goals of a liberal education are less explicit.

THE OVERALL DEVELOPMENT OF THE INVISIBLE COLLEGES

The mortality rate of invisible colleges cannot be documented accurately because the records of so many now-defunct colleges have been lost. It has been estimated that over 2,000 colleges were founded during the nineteenth century, and that only 20 percent of them survived (Patillo & MacKenzie, 1966). Some died because of their poor locations, others because of internal dissension, others because of natural disasters such as fires or tornadoes, and still others because students simply did not enroll in them (Brubacher & Rudy, 1958). The survivors are still just hanging on.

As the nature of higher education has changed in America, the invisible college too has changed. It has been forced to make at least superficial adaptations, and often the pressure for further revisions is pervasive on the campus. Twelve percent of the invisible colleges, for instance, have undergone name changes that reflect a shift from a sectarian to a nonsectarian emphasis. For instance, the institution that was originally founded as Arkansas Christian College now calls itself Harding College. Whatever the reason for this new nomenclature, the result is that the college now appears to be less interested in providing a rigid Christian education and more interested in appealing to a wider range of students, Christian and non-Christian alike.

Often a name change reflects a school's desire to expand its curriculum from a specific area of study to a more comprehensive program. Berry College in Georgia is an instance of an industrial school (originally called Boys' Industrial School) that expanded into the liberal arts, a curricular change that necessitated a new designation. Since many invisible colleges that started out as technical schools have been forced to expand in similar ways, usually to boost student enrollment, they are more likely to have undergone a name change than have the elite colleges, which were oriented toward the liberal arts from their inception. Other invisible colleges that changed their names include a school that expanded from a two-year to a four-year program, schools that merged, men's and women's colleges that became coeducational, and, of course, schools that severed their religious ties altogether.

A college that drops its religious affiliation, changes to a coeducational college, expands its goals from vocational or teacher training to general liberal arts, or moves from one location to another bears little resemblance to the college its founders had in mind. It also has little chance of becoming better known because its image in the academic community keeps shifting. Although such individual developments may seem trivial at first, they take on significance when they characterize an entire group of colleges. The invisible colleges are in a constant state of flux, and their turmoil is not simply a matter of minor revisions in curriculum or internal governance but of fundamental change, change that relates to their whole raison d'être. Unlike the elite colleges, their ability to survive has always been in question. It is difficult to live from day to day in such doubt. The changes that they have undergone reflect their desire to survive and indeed their ability to change in order to survive.

The primary concern of all these private colleges—both sectarian and nonsectarian—was, and still is, survival, especially given the trend in the United States towards nonsectarian, state-supported, tuition-free higher education for all.

3. Administrative Characteristics

More than half of all higher educational institutions in the United States are privately controlled. Of the four-year colleges, nearly two-thirds are private. Since at least half of these private colleges have enrollments of under 2,500 and students whose mean SATs are below 1,000, invisible colleges make up approximately *one-third* of all four-year institutions in the United States. They account for proportionately fewer students because of their relatively small sizes; but nonetheless, they enroll nearly half a million students, or about 15 percent of all students attending four-year institutions. In short, their influence is widespread enough to merit our attention.

In this chapter, we shall examine the demographic and administrative characteristics of the invisible colleges: their geographic distribution, religious affiliation, race and sex, admissions requirements, tuition and financial aid, faculty and library resources, and finances. To provide a context for these facts, our 494 invisible colleges will be compared simultaneously with 44 elite colleges, with the "middle" group of 380 private colleges (which, by our definition, are neither elite nor invisible and which will hereafter be referred to as the *middle colleges*), and, on occasion, with the entire population of 2,319 institutions. Most of our information comes from the files of the U.S. Office of Education and applies to the academic years 1966–67 and 1967–68. Data on finances, which are presented in the last section, were obtained from *American Universities and Colleges* (Singletary, 1968) and from *American Junior Colleges* (Gleazer, 1967).

GEOGRAPHIC DISTRIBUTION The geographic distributions of the four groups of institutions are shown in Table 6. Compared with higher educational institutions in general, invisible colleges are somewhat overrepresented in the

	Invisible colleges (N = 494)	Elite colleges (N = 44)	Other private 4-year colleges (N = 380)	All higher educational institutions (N = 2,319)
Region				
Northeast	21.7	70.5	42.1	28.4
Midwest	35.4	13.6	29.5	27.9
Southeast	26.7	4.5	13.9	22.4
West-Southwest	16.2	11.4	14.5	21.2

TABLE 6 Geographic distribution of the three types of private colleges (percentages)

SOURCE: U.S. Office of Education, 1968*b*.

Midwest and the Southeast and somewhat underrepresented in the Northeast and West-Southwest, though all three groups of private four-year colleges are underrepresented in the last of these regions.

The geographic distribution of elite colleges contrasts markedly with that of the invisible colleges: elite colleges are greatly over-represented in the Northeast and greatly underrepresented in the Midwest and, to an even greater extent, in the Southeast. The middle colleges occupy a middle ground, being overrepresented in the Northeast, underrepresented in the Southeast, and about proportionately represented in the Midwest. As we shall see subsequently, the middle colleges occupy a midposition between invisible and elite colleges in many (but by no means all) comparisons. The tendency for the three groups to be rank-ordered as elite, middle, invisible reinforces the notion that institutional visibility is a continuum.

An additional fact worth noting is that the geographic distribution of invisible colleges is closer to that of institutions in general than is the geographic distribution of either elite or middle institutions. As a matter of fact, all but three states (Delaware, Nevada, and Wyoming) have at least one invisible college; no other type of institution—public two-year colleges, private two-year colleges, public universities, private universities, or even the middle group of private colleges—has such a wide geographic representation. In a sense, then, this study deals with a problem in higher education that is national in scope, more so perhaps than is the case with any other subgroup of institutions.

Is the distribution of invisible, elite, and middle colleges similar in states within a given region? Although the number of institutions in many states is too small for reliable comparisons, Table 7 shows the distribution of the three types of college in the 17 states that have at least 50 higher educational institutions. The percentages shown in each column of Table 7 can be evaluated by comparing them with the percentage for all states, which is given in the first row. For example, invisible colleges appear to be most highly represented in Indiana, Tennessee, and Wisconsin. Elite colleges, on the other hand, are most highly represented in Massachusetts, New York, Ohio, and Pennsylvania. The middle colleges are most highly represented in Minnesota, New York, Ohio, and Pennsylvania.

The relative predominance of invisible colleges over the other two types of private colleges provides a rough inverse measure of the prestige and affluence of a state's private system of higher education. Invisible colleges outnumber other types of private colleges by a ratio of more than 2 to 1 in six states: Iowa, Michigan, Missouri, North Carolina, Tennessee, and Wisconsin. It would seem that private higher education in these states is much more in need of support than it is in states like Massachusetts, Minnesota, New

TABLE 7 *Distribution of the three types of private colleges among states having at least 50 higher educational institutions*

State	Total institutions in state	Percent institutions in state that are:		
		Invisible colleges	Elite colleges	Other 4-year private colleges
(All states)	(2,319)	(21.3)	(1.9)	(16.4)
California	174	15.5	2.3	17.2
Florida	51	15.7	2.0	13.7
Illinois	104	20.2	0.0	24.0
Indiana	50	36.0	0.0	24.0
Iowa	55	30.9	1.8	14.5
Massachusetts	97	14.4	6.2	21.6
Michigan	80	26.3	0.0	12.5
Minnesota	52	15.4	1.9	26.9
Missouri	61	31.1	0.0	14.8
New York	184	13.0	3.3	29.3
North Carolina	77	24.7	1.3	7.8
Ohio	93	23.7	3.2	25.8
Pennsylvania	148	15.5	4.7	29.1
Tennessee	50	46.0	0.0	12.0
Texas	105	20.0	0.0	7.6
Virginia	59	13.6	0.0	16.9
Wisconsin	53	32.1	1.9	9.4

SOURCE: U.S. Office of Education, 1968*b*.

York, and Pennsylvania, where elite and middle colleges outnumber invisible colleges by nearly 2 to 1.

Two states not shown in Table 7 — Connecticut and Maine — each have three elite colleges, representing 8 and 14 percent, respectively, of the private colleges in these states. Although the proportion of invisible colleges in Connecticut is only 5 percent, in Maine, it is 29 percent.

Very high proportions of invisible colleges are located in two other states not shown in Table 7: Kentucky (47 percent) and New Hampshire (56 percent). Kentucky is of particular interest since its pattern is almost identical to that of Tennessee, its neighbor to the south. The case of New Hampshire is a striking one, for in most other Northeastern states elite and middle colleges predominate over invisible colleges.

In summary, although there are considerable numbers of invisible colleges in all regions of the country, the Midwestern and Southeastern states have more than their share. Moreover, individual states, even within the same region, differ greatly in their relative concentrations of invisible as opposed to other types of private colleges. These findings suggest that the condition and needs of private higher education vary substantially by state and by region of the country.

RELIGIOUS AFFILIATIONS The religious affiliations of the four groups of institutions are shown in Table 8. Most striking is the high percentage of nonsectarian institutions among the elite colleges: more than nine in ten of these institutions have no formal religious affiliation. This concentration of nonsectarian institutions exceeds that of our entire population of 2,319 institutions, even though the latter group includes all public institutions (which are, of course, nonsectarian).

With respect to religious affiliation, the middle colleges resemble the invisible colleges much more than they do the elite colleges, although there are some differences. Invisible colleges, for example, are less likely than are the middle colleges to be Roman Catholic, Lutheran, and nonsectarian, and slightly more likely to be Baptist, Southern Baptist, Seventh-Day Adventist, and "other" sects. The four largest denominations (five or more institutions) in this latter group are African Methodist Episcopal, Church of the Nazarene, Church of the Brethren, and Disciples of Christ. Of the 28 institutions in the United States that are affiliated with one of these four denominations, 24 are invisible colleges.

TABLE 8 *Religious affiliations of the three types of private colleges (percentages)*

Denomination	Invisible colleges (N = 494)	Elite colleges* (N = 44)	Other private 4-year colleges (N = 380)	All higher educational institutions (N = 2,319)
Nonsectarian	34.0	90.9	39.7	69.3
Roman Catholic	22.9	4.5	32.1	12.9
American Lutheran	0.4	0.0	1.6	0.4
American Baptist	3.2	0.0	1.8	1.3
Church of Christ	1.0	0.0	0.0	0.6
Lutheran Church	1.0	0.0	3.7	1.0
Methodist	6.1	0.0	6.6	3.3
Presbyterian (U.S.)	4.0	4.5	5.0	2.0
Southern Baptist	5.5	0.0	1.3	2.0
Seventh-Day Adventist	1.8	0.0	0.3	0.5
Other religions	20.1	0.1	7.9	6.7

*While only four elite colleges listed themselves in the Office of Education files as having religious affiliations, other sources say different. For example, Cass and Birnbaum, *Comparative Guide to American Colleges and Universities, 1970–71 Edition,* lists three others as having ties with a religious sect: one to the Society of Friends, one to the Methodist Church, and one to the Presbyterian Church. Thus the invisible colleges are not the only schools that feel ambivalent about their church affiliation; some elite colleges are equally ambivalent. But most of them have severed their previous sectarian ties and, to a large extent, have been in the vanguard of the movement toward nonsectarianism in private higher education.

SOURCE: U.S. Office of Education, 1968b.

These findings show clearly that one of the major distinguishing characteristics of invisibility is affiliation with a religious denomination. Whereas Roman Catholic institutions appear to be more heavily concentrated among the middle colleges than among the invisible colleges, three of the major Protestant denominations — Lutheran, Methodist, and Presbyterian — are about equally represented among these two groups but underrepresented among the elite colleges (the one exception here being the Presbyterians, where the proportions are similar for all three types). The Baptists and the smaller fundamentalist sects, however, are much more heavily represented among the invisible than among the middle colleges and are not found in the elite group at all.

As has already been pointed out in Chapter 2, statistics on the nonsectarianism of invisible colleges can often be misleading. Some of the invisible colleges designate themselves as both nonsectarian (in the Office of Education files) and as members of a religious sect (in, for instance, the *Southern Baptist Directory of Colleges*). Of the 163 invisible colleges that designated themselves as "nonsectarian" with the Office of Education, 60 of them were discovered to be religiously affiliated, as indicated by religious directories or by their catalogs. Some of these colleges were interdenominational, others were active members of a single religious sect.

This kind of dual self-characterization underscores the trend toward nonsectarianism in higher education: colleges are fearful that if they list themselves with the federal government as sectarian, it will be more difficult for them to obtain funds. Their fears are not necessarily borne out by the funding habits of the Office of Education, but to some of these colleges, the risk of forgoing funds because of religious ties is not worth taking. Yet, at the same time, they are not ready to sever ties with the church that founded them, regardless of how strong the trend toward nonsectarianism becomes.

RACE AND SEX Table 9 shows the distribution of predominantly black institutions among our four groups. By *predominantly black* is meant institutions identified by the U.S. Office of Education as enrolling at least 50 percent black students. (The vast majority of these institutions actually enroll close to 100 percent blacks.) About half of all black institutions in the United States (46 of 93) are private colleges and, of these, all but two are invisible colleges. (The two black colleges in the middle group missed being classified as invisible because their enrollments were above 2,500.) In short, for all practical purposes, any black private college can be considered invisible almost by definition. In this sense, then, the private black colleges in the United States can be considered as one subgroup among the invisible colleges.

The sex (men's, women's, coeducational) of the four groups is shown in Table 10. While three out of every four invisible colleges

TABLE 9 *Predominantly black institutions among the three types of private colleges*

Predominantly black institutions	Invisible colleges (N = 494)	Elite colleges (N = 44)	Other private 4-year colleges (N = 380)	All higher educational institutions (N = 2,319)
Number	44	0	2	93
Percentage	8.9	0.0	0.5	4.0

SOURCE: U.S. Office of Education, 1968b.

TABLE 10 *Men's, women's, and coeducational institutions among the three types of private colleges (percentages)*

Sex of college	Invisible colleges (N = 494)	Elite colleges (N = 44)	Other private 4-year colleges (N = 380)	All higher educational institutions (N = 2,319)
Coeducational	75.1	40.9	59.2	81.8
Men only	7.3	38.6	16.6	7.0
Women only	17.6	20.5	24.2	11.2

SOURCE: U.S. Office of Education, 1968*b*.

are coeducational, fewer than half of the elite colleges admit both sexes. Once again, the middle colleges fall in between the elite and the invisible groups.

To some extent the data in Table 10 are misleading, in that the discrepancies would be even greater if Roman Catholic institutions were tabulated separately. A large majority of the noncoeducational invisible colleges are Roman Catholic, whereas only a few of the elite noncoeducational institutions have that affiliation. In other words, looking only at Protestant and nonsectarian private colleges, one finds that more than 95 percent of the invisible colleges, as compared with less than half of the elite colleges, are coeducational. It should be added, however, that the current trend—especially among elite institutions—is to change from noncoeducational to coeducational status.

ADMISSIONS AND ENROLLMENTS Table 11 indicates the admissions requirements of the four groups of institutions. Fewer than half of the invisible colleges (43 percent) require their applicants to take the College Entrance Examination

TABLE 11 *Admissions requirements of the three types of private colleges (percentages)*

Requirements	Invisible colleges (N = 494)	Elite colleges (N = 44)	Other private 4-year colleges (N = 380)	All higher educational institutions (N = 2,319)
CEEB Scholastic Aptitude Test (SAT)	42.9	97.7	91.1	44.7
CEEB Achievement Tests	12.3	84.1	41.9	18.9
ACT Tests	30.4	0.0	13.7	28.0
B or better average in high school	67.8	100.0	97.9	76.8

SOURCE: U.S. Office of Education, 1968*b*.

Board's Scholastic Aptitude Test (SAT), as against all but one (98 percent) of the elite colleges. An even greater difference between these two groups appears in the figures for requirement of the CEEB achievement tests: 12 percent of the invisible colleges versus 84 percent of the elite colleges. Conversely, nearly one-third of the invisible colleges, but *none* of the elite colleges, requires the American College Testing Program (ACT) tests of its applicants.

This contrast in large degree reflects the history of the two testing programs: the College Entrance Examination Board and the American College Testing Program. The College Entrance Examination Board, the older of the two organizations, has traditionally served the elite institutions, especially those located in the Northeastern states. The American College Testing Program was established primarily to fill the gap represented by the junior colleges and the lesser-known private four-year colleges. The middle colleges resemble the elite colleges more than they do the invisible colleges in their preference for the CEEB over the ACT program.

The last row in Table 11 shows the percentage of each group of institutions that requires entering students to have at least a B average in secondary school. (These admissions standards and requirements were reported by each institution on a form distributed by the American Council on Education in connection with the compilation of data for Singletary's *American Universities and Colleges,* 1968.) All the elite colleges, nearly all the middle colleges, but only two-thirds of the invisible colleges reported that applicants must have at least a B average to be considered for admission. But, as we shall see in the next chapter, there is some question about whether even this proportion of the invisible colleges actually recruits student bodies that meet this relatively low standard.

Table 12 shows the distribution of full-time students among all four groups of institutions. All three types of private colleges admit primarily full-time students, although the invisible colleges and the middle colleges are more likely to enroll substantial proportions of part-time students than are the elite colleges. More than 90 percent of the elite colleges enroll at least 90 percent of their students on a full-time basis, as compared with only about half of the invisible colleges and the middle colleges. The reasons for this difference are not entirely clear. Perhaps the elite colleges, because of their large applicant pools and high ratios of applications to acceptances, can afford to require that all students attend on a full-time basis, whereas the less affluent institutions often find it neces-

TABLE 12   *Distribution of full-time students among the three types of private colleges (percentages)*

% of students attending full-time	Invisible colleges (N = 494)	Elite colleges (N = 44)	Other private 4-year colleges (N = 380)	All higher educational institutions (N = 2,319)
Less than 50	4.2	0.0	6.3	4.0
50–54	2.6	2.3	3.2	1.6
55–59	2.8	0.0	2.4	2.4
60–64	2.4	0.0	5.8	2.8
65–69	3.0	0.0	6.6	3.6
70–74	4.7	0.0	5.3	3.2
75–79	6.3	2.3	6.8	4.5
80–84	9.1	0.0	4.5	4.5
85–89	13.8	4.5	7.9	8.1
90–94	16.0	11.4	11.3	10.9
95–98	19.6	31.8	22.1	23.5
99–100	15.4	47.7	17.9	30.8

SOURCE: U.S. Office of Education, 1968*b*.

sary to accept students on a part-time basis in order to fill the places available. Another possible explanation is that the home of the typical invisible college student is closer to his institution (see Chapter 4), making part-time attendance more likely for him than for the elite college student, who typically travels far from home and lives on campus.

The percentages of foreign students enrolled in each of the three groups of private institutions and in all higher education institutions are shown in Table 13. Clearly, the elite colleges are much

TABLE 13   *Distribution of foreign students as a percentage of full-time enrollment*

Percentage	Invisible colleges (N = 494)	Elite colleges (N = 44)	Other private 4-year colleges (N = 380)	All higher educational institutions (N = 2,319)
0	47.8	11.4	22.4	53.6
1–4	43.5	81.8	67.4	39.7
5–9	5.5	2.3	6.6	4.7
10–14	1.6	2.3	1.8	1.0
15 or more	1.6	2.3	2.0	1.0

SOURCE: U.S. Office of Education, 1968*b*.

more likely to enroll foreign students than are the invisible colleges: only 11 percent of the elite colleges, as compared with nearly half of the invisible colleges, enroll no foreign students. Once again, we find the middle group of private colleges equidistant between the invisible and the elite colleges. The relatively low concentration of foreign students in the invisible colleges is probably attributable to several factors. For one thing, their very invisibility makes it unlikely that a foreign student would be aware of their existence; for another, their lack of facilities, scholarships, and special programs for foreign students render them less attractive. Nevertheless, over half of the invisible colleges enroll *some* foreign students.

TUITION AND FINANCIAL AID Data on tuitions charged by the four groups of institutions are given in Table 14. Here one finds one of the largest gaps between the invisible and the elite colleges: 93 percent of the elite group, as compared with less than 4 percent of the invisible colleges, charge at least $1,500 tuition. Moreover, these figures are based on the academic year 1967–68, and there is good reason to believe that the gap has widened even more since then. Independent research (Astin & Holland, 1962) has shown that the higher the tuition charged by an institution, the more likely it is to increase over time. In order to test this possibility within the current study, we consulted several college guides to determine what tuition was charged by invisible and elite colleges in 1968 and in 1970 (Figure 2). Not surprisingly, both groups made substantial tuition increases during that time span. Although the *percentage* increase was slightly higher for

TABLE 14 *Annual tuitions of the three types of private colleges (percentages)*

Annual tuition (out-of-state)	Invisible colleges (N = 494)	Elite colleges (N = 44)	Other private 4-year colleges (N = 380)	All higher educational institutions (N = 2,319)
Less than $300	1.0	0.0	0.8	5.7
$300–$500	3.0	0.0	1.3	15.7
$501–$750	17.8	0.0	5.3	25.8
$751–$1,000	41.3	0.0	16.6	22.1
$1,001–$1,500	33.0	6.8	52.6	20.6
$1,501–$2,000	3.4	81.8	20.8	8.4
$2,000 or more	0.4	11.4	2.6	1.7

SOURCE: U.S. Office of Education, 1968*b*.

FIGURE 2 *Changes in mean tuition for invisible and elite colleges between 1968 and 1970*

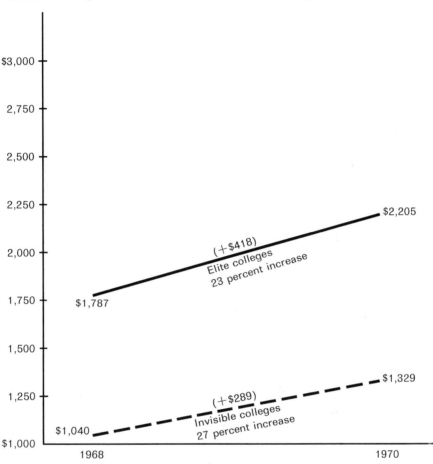

invisible colleges (27 percent versus 23 percent for the elite colleges), the *absolute* dollar increase was substantially higher for the elite colleges ($418 versus $289 in the invisible colleges). In short, the gaps in tuition (and therefore in income) between elite and invisible colleges are widening. Clearly, because of their greater appeal to the prospective student, the elite colleges are in a much better position than are the invisible colleges to charge high tuitions and to make tuition increases palatable.

It is important to point out that, even though he pays a relatively low tuition charge, the student at an invisible college still must pay more to obtain his college education than he would pay at most public institutions. In 1967–68, nearly one-fourth of all higher educational institutions (mostly the public ones) charged less than $500 tuition, as compared with only 4 percent of the invisible colleges. If one considers the minimal tuition charges that public institutions require of residents of the state (only out-of-state tuition charges are given in Table 14), the proportion of institutions charging less than $500 is increased considerably.

In short, the invisible college is caught in a bind between the elite colleges, which are able to charge high tuition fees because of their popularity with prospective students, and the public institutions, which lack the prestige of the elite colleges but can attract students because of their very low fees. The middle group of private colleges is probably subject to some of the same pressures but not to as severe a degree as the invisible colleges.

Table 15 shows the percentages of full-time students at each of the three groups of private colleges, and at all higher education institutions, who receive scholarships from the institution. One-third of the invisible colleges are apparently unable to offer scholarships to any of their students, as compared with only 5 percent of the elite colleges and 6 percent of the middle colleges. Surprisingly enough, however, the proportion of institutions that are able to provide scholarship aid to at least 40 percent of their students is about the same (9 percent) for all three groups of private colleges. This rela-

TABLE 15 *Distribution of scholarship recipients among the three types of private colleges (percentages)*

% of full-time students with scholarships	Invisible colleges (N = 494)	Elite colleges (N = 44)	Other private 4-year colleges (N = 380)	All higher educational institutions (N = 2,319)
0	34.2	4.5	5.8	28.5
1–9	12.0	0.0	15.0	29.9
10–19	19.0	18.2	29.5	19.8
20–29	16.4	31.8	26.3	11.3
30–39	9.2	36.3	13.2	5.4
40–49	4.0	4.5	6.6	2.5
50–59	1.8	0.0	2.9	1.1
60–69	1.4	4.6	0.6	0.7
70–79	1.0	0.0	0.0	0.4
80–89	0.4	0.0	0.0	0.1
90–100	0.6	0.0	0.3	0.4

SOURCE: U.S. Office of Education, 1968*b*.

TABLE 16 *Distributions of student loan funds among the three types of private colleges (percentages)*

% of full-time students given loans	Invisible colleges (N = 494)	Elite colleges (N = 44)	Other private 4-year colleges (N = 380)	All higher educational institutions (N = 2,319)
0	36.6	6.8	10.0	35.3
1–9	11.6	9.1	27.6	24.7
10–19	20.6	52.3	36.3	22.1
20–29	15.2	27.3	17.7	10.3
30–39	9.1	2.3	6.6	4.4
40–49	3.0	2.3	0.8	1.3
50–59	1.6	0.0	0.8	0.8
60–69	1.4	0.0	0.3	0.5
70–79	0.4	0.0	0.0	0.2
80–89	0.0	0.0	0.0	0.1
90–100	0.4	0.0	0.0	0.2

SOURCE: U.S. Office of Education, 1968*b*.

tively high figure for the invisible colleges is accounted for in part by the black colleges, which generally are able to award scholarships to substantial numbers of their students (see Chapter 4).

Data on student loans are shown in Table 16. The pattern here is similar to the one for scholarships: a much higher proportion of the invisible colleges than of the other two groups of private colleges provide no student loans, and yet the number who are in a position to grant loans to a high percentage (above 30 percent) of their students is substantial. As a matter of fact, 16 percent of the invisible colleges (in contrast to only 5 percent of the elite colleges) lend money to at least 30 percent of their students. The middle colleges fall roughly equidistant between the other two with respect to student loans.

Table 17 shows the data on the percentages of students who get jobs through the institution. The pattern of differences is not the same for this kind of student aid as for scholarship and loan aid. Thus, while the proportion that offers no job opportunities is higher for the invisible colleges, it does not work out—as was the case with scholarships and loans—that a relatively high concentration of invisible institutions are able to offer jobs to substantial numbers of their students. Moreover, the middle colleges do not in this in-

TABLE 17 *Distribution of job opportunities among the three types of private colleges (percentages)*

% of full-time students who get jobs through the college	Invisible colleges (N = 494)	Elite colleges (N = 44)	Other private 4-year colleges (N = 380)	All higher educational institutions (N = 2,319)
0	37.2	20.5	10.8	36.7
1–9	8.1	6.8	19.5	20.0
10–19	20.4	15.9	30.0	20.8
20–29	13.4	13.6	21.3	11.1
30–39	11.0	25.0	11.3	6.5
40–49	4.4	4.6	4.0	2.5
50–59	3.0	9.0	1.6	1.3
60–69	0.8	0.0	0.0	0.3
70–79	0.8	2.3	0.0	0.3
80–89	0.2	2.3	0.3	0.2
90–100	0.6	0.0	0.6	0.3

SOURCE: U.S. Office of Education, 1968*b*.

stance occupy a middle ground between the invisible and the elite groups.

In summary, the invisible colleges, as compared with the two other types of private colleges, not only receive less income through tuition but also are less able to make various kinds of financial aid available to their students. It should be stressed, however, that these data are drawn from the 1966–67 academic year and so may not reflect the full impact of various aid programs under the Higher Education Act of 1965. Thus, it is conceivable that more recent figures would reveal smaller discrepancies between the elite and the invisible colleges with respect to financial aid for students. In the next chapter, data based on the entering freshmen of fall 1969 are presented. They suggest that the amount of scholarship aid available to students is about the same in the three types of private colleges.

ACADEMIC RESOURCES   Table 18 shows the percentages of faculty holding doctoral degrees in the four groups of institutions. At only 2 percent of the invisible colleges do at least half the faculty members have the Ph.D. or its equivalent, a sharp contrast to the elite group, in which more than three-fourths of the institutions have faculties where at least half the members have the doctorate. As a matter of fact, *nearly one-third of the invisible colleges have faculties where none of the members has a doctor's degree.* Even among the middle group, only 3 percent have no doctoral degree recipients on their faculties. Nevertheless, it should be pointed out that in more than half of the 494 invisible institutions, at least 20 percent of the faculty hold doctorates.

Obviously, the level of formal academic training of the typical faculty member at an invisible college is far below that of the typical elite college faculty member and is even substantially lower than that of the faculty at the middle colleges. These differences are no doubt a consequence of several factors that characterize the invisible colleges, including their very limited financial resources (see next section on finances) and their lack of prestige in the academic world. As faculty salaries and the general cost of higher education continue to escalate, the bargaining position of the invisible college with respect to recruiting Ph.D.-level faculty is sure to worsen.

The limitations of the invisible colleges' academic resources are made vivid when one compares the size of their libraries with those

TABLE 18 *Distribution of faculty with doctoral degrees among the three types of private colleges (percentages)*

% of faculty holding doctoral degrees	Invisible colleges (N = 494)	Elite colleges (N = 44)	Other private 4-year colleges (N = 380)	All higher educational institutions (N = 2,319)
0	32.4	0.0	2.6	23.1
1–9	3.8	2.3	2.1	24.1
10–19	14.0	0.0	6.5	7.9
20–29	30.0	2.3	22.7	16.0
30–39	15.0	4.6	30.8	12.8
40–49	2.8	13.7	20.6	7.5
50–59	1.2	22.8	11.3	5.0
60–69	0.2	34.1	2.7	2.3
70–79	0.2	15.9	0.8	0.8
80–89	0.4	2.3	0.0	0.3
90–100	0.0	2.3	0.0	0.1

SOURCE: U.S. Office of Education, 1968*b*.

TABLE 19 *Library sizes of the three types of private colleges (percentages)*

Volumes in the library	Invisible colleges (N = 494)	Elite colleges (N = 44)	Other private 4-year colleges (N = 380)	All higher educational institutions (N = 2,319)
Less than 10,000	2.2	0.0	0.8	9.3
10,000–14,999	1.6	0.0	0.0	15.0
15,000–24,999	3.6	4.5	1.6	8.9
25,000–39,999	27.1	2.3	9.2	10.9
40,000–49,999	33.6	0.0	10.0	10.7
50,000–59,999	12.6	2.3	12.4	7.5
60,000–69,999	8.1	2.3	10.8	7.8
70,000–99,999	7.5	0.0	25.3	8.5
100,000–199,999	3.2	25.0	24.5	10.7
200,000–499,999	0.2	52.3	5.3	6.0
500,000–999,999	0.2	9.1	0.3	2.8
1,000,000 or more	0.2	2.3	0.0	1.9

SOURCE: U.S. Office of Education, 1968*b*.

of the other two groups of private colleges (Table 19). Nearly two-thirds of the invisible colleges have fewer than 50,000 books in their libraries. Only 7 percent of the elite colleges and 20 percent of the middle colleges have such small libraries. Conversely, we find that nearly 90 percent of the elite colleges, but only 4 percent of the invisible colleges, have libraries containing as many as 100,000 books. Once again the middle colleges fall in between, with about 30 percent having libraries containing at least 100,000 books.

Table 20 shows the residence hall capacities of the four groups of institutions. Fully one-third of the invisible colleges are unable to provide housing for any of their students. But in all three groups some colleges (though they may constitute a very small minority) can house all their students.

It is worth remarking that all three groups of private colleges, including the invisible ones, can provide housing for a larger proportion of their students than can the typical college in the population (see the last column of Table 20).

FINANCES   Perhaps the most important single index of an institution's financial resources is the amount it spends for educational and general purposes, a category that includes funds spent for faculty and staff salaries, for financial aid to students, and for the general maintenance and operation of the institution. Salaries paid to faculty and staff—the item that ordinarily constitutes the largest expenditure— are a function of the total number of faculty and their average salaries. Consequently, if the educational and general expenditures are expressed on a per-student basis, relatively high expenditures can be interpreted to indicate a high faculty-student ratio, a high pay scale, or (as is typically the case) both.

The per-student education and general expenditures of the three groups of private institutions are shown in Table 21. Because of the great public interest in the comparative costs of public and private institutions, we have also included data for three types of public institutions as well as for all institutions. That every one of our 44 elite colleges spends over $2,500 per student for educational and general purposes is an indication that this scale should have been extended beyond $2,500 to get a more accurate picture. Nevertheless, the data make it clear that invisible colleges spend substantially less money per student for educational and general purposes than does either the elite or middle group of private colleges; more than half of the invisible colleges spend less than

TABLE 20 *Capacity of the residence halls of the three types of private colleges (percentages)*

Percentage of student body that can be accommodated	Invisible colleges (N = 494)	Elite colleges (N = 44)	Other private 4-year colleges (N = 380)	All higher educational institutions (N = 2,319)
0	35.2	0.0	8.2	39.6
1–9	0.0	0.0	0.3	2.0
10–19	1.2	0.0	3.6	3.4
20–29	2.8	0.0	4.8	4.6
30–39	1.8	2.3	6.0	5.2
40–49	5.4	9.1	7.1	6.4
50–59	8.7	6.8	10.8	7.7
60–69	11.6	11.4	16.9	8.6
70–79	9.4	6.8	12.6	6.5
80–89	11.6	18.2	11.6	6.0
90–99	7.0	29.5	7.3	4.4
100	5.3	15.9	10.8	5.6

SOURCE: U.S. Office of Education, 1968*b*.

TABLE 21
Expenditures per student for educational and general purposes at various types of institutions (percentages)

Dollars per student	Invisible colleges (N = 494)	Elite colleges (N = 44)	Other private 4-yr. colleges (N = 380)
Less than 750	0.6	0.0	0.5
751–1,000	1.6	0.0	1.1
1,001–1,250	3.6	0.0	3.2
1,251–1,500	7.5	0.0	2.1
1,501–1,750	9.7	0.0	7.9
1,751–2,000	16.6	0.0	12.6
2,001–2,250	26.7	0.0	15.0
2,251–2,500	6.7	0.0	12.1
More than 2,500	26.9	100.0	45.5

SOURCE: U.S. Office of Education, 1968*b*.

$2,000 per student, and more than 10 percent spend less than $1,500. The concentration of institutions with very low expenditures is nearly as great among middle colleges, although substantially more of them fall in the over $2,500 category. On this characteristic, then, the middle group of private colleges is extremely heterogeneous.

Per-student expenditures in the invisible colleges tend to be somewhat higher than those in public two-year and four-year colleges, although they are not appreciably different from those in the public universities. Public two-year colleges clearly spend less per student than any other group shown in Table 21; in this respect, the invisible colleges bear a closer resemblance to the public four-year colleges than to the public two-year colleges.

It is likely that the per-student expenditures of the invisible colleges are very much affected by their small size. With moderate increases in enrollment, the current level (median of approximately $2,100 per student) might be lowered to the level of expenditures in the public four-year colleges (median of approximately $1,650 per student). About 20 percent of the invisible colleges, of course, already have per-student expenditures that are below the median for public four-year colleges.

Although endowments are steadily becoming a less important source of finances for private institutions, they nevertheless provide a form of "hard" money that is virtually unavailable from other sources. Table 22 shows the per-student book value of the

Public 4-year colleges (N = 323)	Public 2-year colleges (N = 535)	Public universities (N = 72)	All higher educational institutions (N = 2,319)
3.7	25.4	3.6	7.9
2.8	45.8	0.9	12.5
11.1	11.4	2.2	10.1
20.4	8.4	2.7	8.0
18.6	2.2	0.9	7.4
21.7	3.4	46.4	15.3
8.0	0.6	4.0	10.3
3.1	0.9	5.8	5.0
10.5	1.9	33.5	23.4

endowment of the three groups of private colleges and of institutions as a whole. These figures highlight the very limited financial resources of many invisible colleges. Over half of them (61 percent) have per-student endowments below $1,000, as compared with only 16 percent of the elite colleges and 42 percent of the middle colleges. More than half of the elite colleges, in contrast, have

TABLE 22 *Book value of endowments at the three types of private colleges (percentages)*

Dollars per student	Invisible colleges (N = 494)	Elite colleges (N = 44)	Other private 4-year colleges (N = 380)	All higher educational institutions (N = 2,319)
Less than 500	20.4	9.1	23.2	33.9
501–1,000	40.9	6.8	19.2	28.1
1,001–1,400	7.1	2.3	8.4	5.7
1,401–1,600	2.2	0.0	2.4	2.0
1,601–1,800	2.6	0.0	2.9	1.3
1,801–2,000	2.8	2.3	4.2	9.0
2,001–2,200	4.0	0.0	2.6	5.5
2,201–2,600	2.6	6.8	5.0	1.9
2,601–3,000	9.5	2.3	4.2	3.0
3,001–4,500	2.8	13.6	10.0	3.5
More than 4,500	4.9	56.8	17.9	6.3

SOURCE: U.S. Office of Education, 1968*b*.

endowment funds amounting to more than $4,500 per student; only 5 percent of the invisible colleges and 18 percent of the middle colleges are as well endowed.

These figures dramatize once again the vast gulf that separates the elite from the invisible colleges. But here too, one should note that there are exceptions: a substantial number of invisible colleges have relatively large endowment funds, and, conversely, several elite colleges have very limited endowments.

Another important indicator of the financial condition of an institution is the value of its physical plant. Table 23 shows the book value of the physical plants of our three groups expressed on a per-student basis. Of all the finance categories, the discrepancies between invisible, middle, and elite colleges are smallest for this one. Indeed, among the three, the elite group has the highest percentage of physical plants valued at less than $1,150 per student. A somewhat different picture emerges if we examine the upper end of the distribution, where the proportion of elite colleges with physical plants valued at more than $6,700 per student exceeds the proportion of invisible colleges by a ratio of almost 2 to 1. However, the middle colleges exceed *both* of the other groups and nearly twice as many of them as invisible colleges have physical plants valued at more than $5,600 per student.

Why do we find this sudden break in the pattern of finances

TABLE 23 *Book value of physical plants at the three types of private colleges (percentages)*

Dollars per student	Invisible colleges (N = 494)	Elite colleges (N = 44)	Other private 4-year colleges (N = 380)	All higher educational institutions (N = 2,319)
0	0.2	0.0	0.0	0.1
1–1,150	2.8	18.2	5.8	6.7
1,151–2,260	4.7	9.1	5.0	8.5
2,261–3,370	7.3	15.9	8.9	18.5
3,371–4,480	29.6	4.5	10.8	25.0
4,481–5,600	26.7	18.2	14.5	14.2
5,601–6,700	14.6	6.8	14.5	9.7
6,701–7,810	5.5	9.1	18.7	7.4
7,811–10,000	8.7	18.2	21.8	9.8
More than 10,000	0.0	0.0	0.0	0.0

SOURCE: U.S. Office of Education, 1968*b*.

TABLE 24 *Revenues from student fees at the three types of private colleges (percentages)*

Dollars per student	Invisible colleges (N = 494)	Elite colleges (N = 44)	Other private 4-year colleges (N = 380)	All higher educational institutions (N = 2,319)
0–100	0.0	0.0	0.3	4.9
101–350	1.8	2.3	1.1	30.3
351–475	1.0	0.0	0.8	5.4
476–600	5.1	0.0	1.1	10.0
601–725	12.3	0.0	2.9	8.2
726–850	20.9	0.0	5.3	6.4
851–975	11.7	0.0	9.2	5.0
976–1,100	33.2	0.0	15.8	10.2
1,101–1,755	12.3	43.2	54.5	15.1
1,755 or more	1.6	54.5	9.2	4.5

SOURCE: U.S. Office of Education, 1968*b*.

when in other instances the rank ordering of elite, middle, and invisible colleges is consistent? One possible explanation is that the elite colleges, being older than the other two types of private colleges, have physical plants whose book value is substantially below their true market value, either because the initial price was much lower than the current market price or because policies of depreciation substantially reduce the book value of capital property over long periods of time. Whatever the explanation, it appears that in the matter of physical plants, the invisible colleges are at less of a disadvantage vis-à-vis the two other types of private colleges than is the case with most of the measures of financial resources.

The remaining tables in this chapter are concerned with sources of income. We have divided these sources into three categories: student fees, research contracts, and student aid funds.

Table 24 shows institutional revenues from student fees. The enormous differences between invisible and elite colleges are once again dramatized by these data: all but one of the 44 elite colleges receive more than $1,100 in revenue from student fees, as compared with only 14 percent of the invisible colleges. In this instance, the middle colleges stand much closer to the elite colleges, with nearly two-thirds of them receiving more than $1,100 per student in revenues from student fees. Despite these differences, invisible colleges still depend much more on such revenues than do higher educational institutions in general (see the last column of Table 24). For example, fully half of all higher educational institutions in the country receive less than $600 per student in revenues from student fees, as compared with only 8 percent of the invisible colleges.

Table 25 shows institutional revenues from research contracts. Although one would not normally expect private colleges to receive substantial amounts of money in this form, one-fourth of the elite colleges receive more than $600 per student from such contracts. Less than 1 percent of the invisible colleges and only 5 percent of the middle group receive as much money from this source.

Revenues from student aid funds are shown in Table 26. Presumably, these revenues are highly dependent on endowment funds. Using the figure of $200 per student as a cut-off point, we find that only 8 percent of the invisible colleges and 14 percent of the middle group exceed this level. By contrast, two-thirds of the elite colleges receive at least $200 per student in revenues from student aid funds. Again, the elite colleges have a substantial competitive advantage over the invisible and middle colleges in that they have the means to attract students by offers of financial aid. Although all three groups of private colleges receive substantially more income from student aid funds than do institutions in general (see the last column of Table 26), this discrepancy is probably

TABLE 25 *Revenues from research contracts at the three types of private colleges (percentages)*

Dollars per student	Invisible colleges (N = 494)	Elite colleges (N = 44)	Other private 4-year colleges (N = 380)	All higher educational institutions (N = 2,319)
0	0.0	0.0	0.0	4.0
1–50	45.5	18.2	35.0	48.8
51–100	24.3	13.6	41.3	15.3
101–205	8.5	11.4	5.5	13.2
206–310	8.9	9.1	6.1	3.8
311–400	0.2	11.4	6.8	4.6
401–500	0.0	9.1	0.0	0.6
501–600	12.3	2.3	0.3	3.4
601–700	0.0	15.9	3.4	3.2
701 or more	0.2	9.1	1.6	3.2

SOURCE: U.S. Office of Education, 1968*b*.

TABLE 26 *Revenues from student aid funds at the three types of private colleges (percentages)*

Dollars per student	Invisible colleges (N = 494)	Elite colleges (N = 44)	Other private 4-year colleges (N = 380)	All higher educational institutions (N = 2,319)
0	0.0	0.0	0.0	0.2
1–25	13.0	2.3	17.9	24.9
26–50	11.1	2.3	12.6	11.7
51–75	10.9	0.0	13.9	16.8
76–100	34.8	4.5	18.9	14.6
101–200	22.5	25.0	22.9	19.8
201–300	4.9	38.6	8.9	8.9
301–400	2.0	13.6	2.1	1.5
401–500	0.2	2.3	1.6	0.6
501 or more	0.6	11.4	1.1	0.9

SOURCE: U.S. Office of Education, 1968*b*.

explained by the heavily subsidized tuition of the public institutions, which obviates the need for extensive endowments for student aid.

In summary, with respect to financial resources the invisible colleges are in a dismal position. They receive far less money from virtually all sources of revenue than do either elite or middle private colleges. Since their very invisibility presents major difficulties in recruiting students and faculty, their relative lack of funds for salaries and financial aid and the favorable competitive position of public and elite private institutions compound their difficulties. Without major infusions of new money, the outlook for many invisible colleges is bleak.

4. The Students

The characteristics of its student body is one of the most significant attributes of any institution. Institutions have traditionally regarded the quality of their students as important, both because it reflects on their own image or reputation and because it is the students who, as alumni, will ultimately provide the principal source of private support for the institution. Of equal importance is the kind of social and intellectual climate that the students themselves create. Recent research (Astin, 1963; Astin,1968a; Astin & Holland, 1961) has suggested that the characteristics of its student body may be the most important single determinant of the academic and interpersonal climate of an institution.

COMPARISON OF INVISIBLE COLLEGE STUDENTS WITH ELITE COLLEGE STUDENTS

Our access to data on entering freshmen collected in the American Council on Education's Cooperative Institutional Research Program (CIRP) (see Astin, Panos, & Creager, 1966) gave us an opportunity to examine in detail the characteristics of students at invisible colleges. One feature of this research program is that each year a detailed student questionnaire is administered to entire entering freshman classes as a national sample of higher educational institutions. From the fall 1969 survey, we identified 40 invisible and 23 elite colleges. Rather than reporting on all 150 questionnaire items, we have selected 18 that bear directly on the concerns of this report; the data on these items are given in Table 27. (See Appendix A for data on individual institutions.) The principal findings from Table 27 are summarized below.

Demographic characteristics Invisible colleges tend to enroll somewhat smaller proportions of young students (under 18 years old) than do elite colleges. The variation among invisible colleges on this variable, however, is considerable, ranging from zero to 14.1 percent.

TABLE 27
*Selected
characteristics
of entering
freshman
classes at 40
invisible and 23
elite colleges*

	Mean	
Selected item	*Invisible*	*Elite*
Demographic characteristics		
Under 18 years old	4.2	10.1
Home is within 50 miles of the college	28.0	11.6
Grew up on a farm	11.2	2.3
Nonwhite	18.5	
Jewish	2.0	11.7
Roman Catholic	38.8	21.7
Father has postgraduate degree	10.6	35.1
Economic characteristics		
Family income below $6,000	20.0	5.4
Scholarship aid is a "major source" of income	28.0	31.1
"Major concern" with finances	14.0	6.5
High school background		
Attended public school	70.9	72.0
High school average of "A"	11.6	50.5
Top 10% of class	25.5	70.3
Degree plans		
Planning Ph.D. degree	10.4	32.0
Planning M.D. degree	3.2	8.6
Planning law degree	0.9	4.8
Political preferences		
Liberal or left	33.1	57.0
Conservative (moderately or strongly)	26.0	17.8

SOURCE: Creager, Astin, Boruch, Bayer, & Drew, 1969.

Responses to an item that asked whether the student's home was within 50 miles of his college revealed that the invisible college student is more likely to attend college close to home, although both invisible and elite colleges are primarily residential. None of the 23 elite colleges recruits even half its students from within 50 miles of the college, whereas six of the 40 invisible colleges recruit more than half their students from within 50 miles. Only one of these institutions, however—Loyola College, Maryland,

Percentage of entering freshmen			
Highest score		Lowest score	
Invisible	Elite	Invisible	Elite
14.1	17.3	0.0	4.7
95.3	43.8	2.6	4.2
55.2	5.2	0.0	0.0
100.0	16.0	0.0	0.0
32.2	26.9	0.0	0.0
94.7	96.3	0.0	8.7
25.9	51.5	1.9	9.1
66.2	8.4	2.3	0.0
65.4	65.2	4.5	16.5
25.6	11.3	1.7	0.0
98.6	90.5	19.0	25.7
31.1	90.4	2.3	25.7
54.8	96.4	7.1	34.9
25.3	87.8	2.4	7.9
10.6	17.4	0.9	0.0
5.0	16.2	0.0	0.0
62.9	88.6	18.0	38.1
52.9	42.9	15.9	3.8

a Catholic college for men located in an urban area —can legitimately be regarded as a commuter college.

In short, the fact that the homes of students attending the typical invisible college tend to be located closer to the college than the homes of students attending the typical elite college is further evidence of the invisible college's poorer drawing power and comparative obscurity.

Substantial differences between invisible and elite colleges are also apparent in the proportions of their students who grew up on a farm. The mean for invisible colleges on this item is 11.2 percent, whereas the *highest* score for any elite college is only 5.2 percent, a figure exceeded by fully two-thirds of the invisible colleges. The students entering the typical invisible college, then, are much more likely to have come from rural backgrounds.

At first glance, it would seem that the typical invisible college enrolls a higher percentage of nonwhites than does the typical elite college. But that first glance is misleading. Five of the forty invisible colleges — but none of the elite colleges — are predominantly black. Thus, if we use medians rather than means to describe the typical elite and invisible college, we find that the median percentage of nonwhites attending invisible colleges is 6.5, as compared to 7.5 for the elite colleges. Thus, of the predominantly white colleges, the typical invisible college enrolls somewhat fewer nonwhites than does the typical elite college.

One interesting additional piece of evidence (not shown in Table 27; see Appendix A) concerns the subgroup of predominantly black colleges among the invisible colleges. The percentage of white students attending four of the five black colleges in this sample was actually zero — no white students were enrolled — and at the fifth, the percentage was 0.4 — one white student was enrolled. At nearly two-thirds of the predominantly white colleges in the invisible group, on the other hand, at least 1 percent of the entering students were black. In short, among the invisible colleges, the most thoroughly segregated are the predominantly black colleges. To be sure, several white colleges enroll very few or no black students, but virtually none of the predominantly black invisible colleges enrolls any white students.

Invisible colleges differ from elite colleges markedly in the proportions of Jewish students among their entering freshmen. The differences in the mean percentages shown in Table 27 are impressive enough (2 percent for invisible colleges, 11.7 percent for elite colleges), but the contrast becomes even more striking when one realizes that the mean percentage for invisible colleges is inflated by the presence in the sample of one private teachers college, located in an urban area, where one-third of the entering students are Jewish. One gets a more accurate picture by looking at the median figures for Jewish students: 0.1 percent at the invisible colleges and 10.1 percent at the elite colleges. In fact, exactly half (20 of 40) of the invisible colleges enroll no Jewish students whatsoever. By contrast, except for the one Catholic college in the elite group (which enrolled no Jews), at least 4 percent of the entering freshman class at every elite college included is Jewish. Only seven of the 40 invisible colleges enrolled as high a percentage.

The differences with respect to the proportion of Roman Catholics attending invisible and elite colleges were less pronounced. Although one may be tempted to conclude that invisible colleges tend to recruit considerably greater concentrations of Roman Catholic students than elite colleges do, it should be kept in mind that the 40 invisible colleges included 12 Roman Catholic institutions, whereas the 23 elite colleges included only one such institution. Consequently, the median percentages of Roman Catholic students among the entering classes are much closer: 24 and 19.2, respectively, for invisible and elite colleges.

The final item of demographic information listed in Table 27 concerns the proportions of students whose fathers had a postgraduate degree (master's, doctoral, or professional). Once again, the two types of institutions contrast sharply. Three times as many students at elite colleges as at invisible colleges reported that their fathers had earned postgraduate degrees. The lowest percentage for any elite college (9.1) still exceeds the percentage for half of the invisible colleges; conversely, the highest percentage for any invisible college (25.9) is exceeded by more than 80 percent of the elite colleges (see Appendix A).

Economic characteristics The first economic variable shown in Table 27 is the proportion of entering students whose family income is below $6,000 per year, a figure arbitrarily selected as a sort of borderline poverty level. Judging by mean percentages, invisible colleges enroll close to four times as many students from families with poverty-level incomes as elite colleges do. Once again, however, these differences are exaggerated by the inclusion in the sample of certain institutions where the percentages are unusually high: in this case, most of the black colleges and a few rural white colleges. Thus, the medians for invisible and elite colleges are closer than the means: 15.6 percent and 5.7 percent, respectively. Even so, the two groups of colleges overlap to only a very small extent. The highest percentage of such poverty-level students enrolled by any elite college is 8.4, a figure exceeded by 85 percent of the invisible colleges.

Despite the substantial differences in their economic backgrounds, roughly the same proportions of students at the two types of institutions receive scholarship aid. The medians are even closer—26.3 percent at the invisible colleges and 27.7 percent at the elite colleges. (This figure, based on student reports, is similar to the one based on institutional reports and mentioned in Chapter 3.) Why is it that, despite their greater financial need, students at invisible colleges are not receiving more scholarship aid than students at elite colleges? This apparent inequity probably has several explanations. For one thing, as we have seen, the financial resources—including internal scholarship funds—of the elite colleges are substantially greater than those of the invisible colleges. Furthermore, one of the major functions of scholarships (as opposed to other forms of financial aid) is to encourage and reward highly talented students. Since students attending the elite colleges are usually the most able academically, we should expect to find substantial numbers of them receiving National Merit Scholarships and other awards from sources external to the institution. Nevertheless, since the amount of such awards is typically based on an assessment of the student's financial need, it is surprising that equal proportions of students in the two types of institutions reported that scholarship money is a major source of income for defraying college expenses.

That the financial aid going to students who attend invisible colleges may not be sufficient to meet their needs is suggested by the next item in Table 27, which shows the percentages of entering students who express "major concern" over financing their college education. Once again we find substantial differences between the two types of institutions: the highest percentage of students at any elite college who indicate anxiety over finances is 11.3, a figure exceeded at nearly two-thirds of the invisible colleges.

High school background From the mean percentages shown in Table 27, it would seem at first that the percentages of students at invisible colleges and at elite colleges who attended public high school are roughly the same. But again, the inclusion of some "special cases" in the small samples of institutions tends to give a distorted impression. If we exclude from consideration the one elite and the 12 invisible Catholic institutions, a somewhat different picture emerges: three-fourths of the 28 non-Catholic invisible colleges enroll at least 85 percent of their students from public high schools, whereas only four of the 22 non-Catholic elite colleges enroll this high a percentage of their freshmen from public high schools. The invisible colleges, then, would seem to have poor drawing power for students who attended non-Catholic private secondary schools.

Comparing the academic records of students at invisible colleges with those of students at elite colleges, we find confirmation for the use of students' mean scores on tests of academic ability as our principal defining criterion for invisibility versus eliteness. The lowest percentage of students with A averages in high school among the elite institutions (25.7) is exceeded by only three of the 40 invisible colleges, whereas the highest percentage of students with A averages at any invisible college (31.1) is exceeded by all but four of the 23 elite colleges. Similar differences appear in the proportions who graduated in the top tenth of their high school class: the highest such percentage among invisible colleges (54.8) is exceeded by all but three of the elite colleges. Aptitude test scores (our major defining variable for invisibility) and high school records, however, cannot be regarded as completely interchangeable measures, since the invisible and the elite colleges overlapped slightly on the two measures of high school achievement — grades and class rank. This overlap probably derives from two factors: the rather stringent grading standards at non-Catholic private secondary schools (which would tend to lower the mean for students at elite colleges) and the presence of the five black colleges (whose entering students tend to have better academic records than do students in other invisible colleges). The black students' grades are, however, still below the grades of students in general. (See, for example, Bayer & Boruch, 1969.)

Educational aspirations The data in Table 27 concerning students' degree plans once more reveal substantial differences between invisible and elite colleges, particularly with respect to the Ph.D. For example, the invisible college where the percentage of students aspiring to the Ph.D. is largest (25.3) still falls below the mean for the elite colleges (32 percent). The elite colleges and the invisible colleges also differ (though less drastically) in the proportions of their entering freshmen who want to get either a medical or a law degree.

The degree aspirations of students enrolling at predominantly black institutions are worth noting. Of the 40 invisible colleges, the five black institutions had the highest proportions of entering freshmen aspiring to the Ph.D. The proportions who said they planned to get the M.D. or LL.B. degrees also tended to be above the average for invisible colleges in general. These findings confirm the results of earlier research (Bayer & Boruch, 1969), which indicates that black students, in spite of their relatively poor academic preparation for college, have educational aspirations that exceed those of the typical white student.

Political preferences   The last two items in Table 27 concern the students' political preferences. For purposes of comparison, students who indicated that their political beliefs were either "liberal" or "left" have been combined into one group, as have students who described themselves as either "strongly conservative" or "moderately conservative." A fifth category, "middle-of-the-road," is not shown.

Students at both types of institutions are more likely to characterize themselves as liberal than as conservative, but this tendency is much more pronounced at elite institutions. In 32 of the 40 invisible colleges and in all but one of the elite colleges,

TABLE 28 *Career choices* *of students at* *40 invisible* *and 23 elite* *colleges*		

TABLE 28
Career choices of students at 40 invisible and 23 elite colleges

Career	Mean	
	Invisible	*Elite*
Artist	6.9	8.4
Businessman	10.0	3.6
Clergyman	1.6	0.5
College teacher	1.5	3.9
Elementary teacher	14.7	1.6
Engineer	1.7	7.1
Farmer or forester	1.4	0.5
Health professional (non-M.D.)	5.1	1.1
Lawyer	2.7	8.0
Nurse	3.5	0.1
Physician (M.D.)	2.7	7.3
Research scientist	2.4	9.4
Secondary teacher	17.2	7.7
Other choice	18.1	18.5
Undecided	10.3	22.3

SOURCE: Creager, Astin, Boruch, Bayer, & Drew, 1969.

liberals outnumber conservatives. If we examine the ratios of liberals to conservatives, the disparity between elite and invisible colleges is much greater. Among the elite colleges, for example, liberals outnumber conservatives by a ratio of at least 2 to 1 in all but two of the 23 institutions; by contrast, at only nine of the 40 invisible colleges do liberals outnumber conservatives to this extent. If we take an even more extreme break—a 3 to 1 ratio of liberals over conservatives—we find that half (12 of 23) of the elite colleges but none of the invisible colleges equal or surpass this ratio. There were, in fact, four elite colleges where the liberal or left students outnumbered conservatives by more than 10 to 1.

Career choice Looking at the invisible colleges with respect to their potential output of trained manpower, as defined by the career choices of their students, and comparing them with the career choices of elite college students (see Table 28), it is immediately apparent that the student at the invisible college is much more pragmatically and vocationally oriented. Furthermore, he is not as likely to aspire to a high-level professional career as is the student at the elite college. For example, 7.3 percent of the

Percentage of entering freshmen			
Highest score		*Lowest score*	
Invisible	*Elite*	*Invisible*	*Elite*
28.5	39.9	0.0	0.0
27.1	12.2	0.0	0.0
7.2	1.3	0.0	0.0
4.5	8.4	0.0	0.0
76.7	5.0	0.0	0.0
6.2	72.7	0.0	0.0
23.0	1.3	0.0	0.0
17.2	3.4	0.0	0.0
9.0	24.4	0.0	0.0
32.8	1.0	0.0	0.0
10.4	16.1	0.0	0.0
14.0	55.6	0.0	0.0
29.3	19.8	3.0	0.0
48.8	39.0	2.1	4.1
27.5	35.7	0.0	0.0

entering freshmen at elite colleges say they plan to become physicians, as against 2.7 percent in the invisible colleges. Similarly, 8 percent of the students in elite colleges plan to become attorneys, compared with only 2.7 percent in the invisible colleges; and 7.1 percent plan to become engineers, as against 1.7 percent in the invisible colleges.

If one accepts the typical values of American society—which define medicine, law, and engineering as three high-status professions—one can make some inferences about the kinds of students attending the invisible colleges: namely, they are approximately one generation behind the students at elite colleges in conventional upward mobility. (This inference is to some degree substantiated by the data in Table 27, which indicates that the typical invisible college student comes from a low socioeconomic background.)

Another approach is to look at those professions which normally are not within the patterns of upward mobility of less affluent families; artist and research scientist are two such professions. At the elite colleges, 8.4 percent of the entering freshmen want to become artists, as compared with 6.9 percent in the invisible colleges; and 9.4 percent want to become research scientists, as compared with 2.4 percent in the invisible colleges. The noteworthy point here is that students in the invisible college seem to shy away from occupations that require postbaccalaureate work. If this is indeed the case, it would explain why the discrepancy between invisible and elite colleges, with respect to the proportions of their freshmen who want to become artists, is relatively small. The various artistic fields, though they may be regarded as nonpragmatic, generally do not require much formal academic training beyond the bachelor's degree.

The data in Table 28 also indicate that students at invisible colleges seem to choose the service professions where the demand is relatively high: elementary and secondary teaching, the non-M.D. health professions, and nursing are many times more popular as career choices with students in the invisible colleges than with those in the elite colleges. Again, consistent with his pragmatic orientation, the invisible college student is almost three times more inclined to plan a career in business. Similarly, even though only 1.6 percent of the invisible college students pick clergyman as a career, this figure exceeds the mean percentage at the elite colleges by 3 to 1.

In general, then, the students at invisible colleges seem to have decidedly different goals from those of students at the elite colleges. It should be borne in mind that this survey was administered at the time the student matriculated, so his career choice probably reflects his self-evaluation as to his own aspirations and abilities. His selection of a particular college may, in turn, have been partially determined by his career choice. Moreover, since the invisible college student is usually not gifted intellectually, he may have been counseled by his parents or teachers not to pursue a career that involves rigorous training. It is also possible that, coming from a lower socioeconomic group, the student at the invisible college finds it impractical to consider careers that require considerable expenditures of money; in addition, his family background might discourage him from making a broad leap upwards on the occupational ladder.

The comparative percentages of students who are undecided about their future careers may reflect the strictures imposed on the students at the invisible colleges; only 10.3 percent say that they are undecided, as against 22.3 percent of the students in the elite colleges, who can better afford to take their time about making up their minds.

To recapitulate briefly: The proportions of students aspiring to high-level professional careers (college teacher, engineer, lawyer, physician, research scientist) are much higher in the elite colleges (35.7 percent) than in the invisible colleges (11 percent), whose students are much more likely to plan careers as businessmen, schoolteachers, farmers, health professionals (non-M.D.), or nurses (51.9 percent, as against 14.6 percent of the students in elite colleges). In short, the invisible colleges deal with a very different kind of clientele than do the elite colleges. Their students are much more practical-minded and much less ambitious in their career plans. The implication here is that the invisible colleges should not try to emulate the model of the elite colleges (as some do). Such a model is completely inappropriate for them in view of the abilities and career plans of their students.

COMPARISON OF INVISIBLE COLLEGE STUDENTS WITH FOUR-YEAR AND TWO-YEAR PUBLIC COLLEGE STUDENTS If freshmen entering invisible colleges differ so drastically from those entering elite colleges, how do they compare with students at the public four-year colleges and the public two-year colleges? Table 29 shows the data on the same 18 selected items as were listed in Table 27, but in this case, mean percentages only have been included, and the comparison groups have been extended to include the following groups of institutions identi-

TABLE 29 *Selected characteristics of entering freshmen at four types of colleges*

	Mean percentage of entering freshmen			
Selected item	Invisible (N = 40)	Public 4-year (N = 21)	Private 2-year (N = 25)	Elite (N = 23)
Demographic characteristics				
Under 18 years old	4.2	5.2	2.3	10.1
Home is within 50 miles of the college	28.0	56.4	87.2	11.6
Grew up on a farm	11.2	11.0	11.2	2.3
Nonwhite	18.5	9.1	10.7	
Jewish	2.0	4.3	1.6	11.7
Roman Catholic	38.8	30.4	38.2	21.7
Father has postgraduate degree	10.6	6.3	3.4	35.1
Economic characteristics				
Family income below $6,000	20.0	15.7	19.1	5.4
Scholarship aid is a "major source" of income	28.0	18.2	12.7	31.1
"Major concern" with finances	14.0	10.6	9.5	6.5
High school background				
Attended public school	70.9	88.6	88.0	72.0
High school average of "A"	11.6	12.5	3.0	50.5
Top 10% of class	25.5	22.6	7.7	70.3
Degree plans				
Planning Ph.D. degree	10.4	9.7	5.0	32.0
Planning M.D. degree	3.2	2.9	2.0	8.6
Planning law degree	0.9	0.8	0.3	4.8
Political preferences				
Liberal or left	33.1	32.8	29.6	57.0
Conservative (moderately or strongly)	26.0	22.3	19.9	17.8

SOURCE: Creager, Astin, Boruch, Bayer, & Drew, 1969.

fied from the Cooperative Institutional Research Program (CIRP) sample: 21 public four-year institutions (state colleges), and 25 public two-year colleges (community colleges). (The figures for the 23 elite colleges are also included, for comparative purposes.)

Demographic characteristics With respect to their demographic characteristics, students at invisible colleges are, on most items, more similar to state college students than to community college students. For instance, the invisible colleges and the public four-year colleges enroll approximately equal proportions of relatively young students (4.2 percent and 5.2 percent, respectively, are under 18), whereas students entering community colleges tend to be older (only 2.3 percent are under 18). On the item asking whether the student's home was within 50 miles of his institution, there are marked differences among the three groups. Twice as many state college students as invisible college students live that close to home, and the figure for community college students is 87.2 percent, which, though high, is not surprising in view of the mission of the community college. In summary, the invisible colleges seem to be more residential than the public colleges, although markedly less so than the elite colleges. The proportions of students at invisible, state, and community colleges who grew up on a farm or in a rural environment are remarkably similar (around 11 percent) and sharply distinct from the proportion at elite colleges (2.3 percent).

Though it would at first appear that invisible colleges enroll more nonwhites than do the two-year and four-year public colleges, one must realize again that the mean percentages are somewhat distorted by the subsample of five virtually all-black institutions in our sample of invisible colleges. The proportionate enrollment of Jewish students at four-year public colleges is twice as great as that at the invisible colleges, which more closely resemble the community colleges in this respect. None of these three groups approaches the elite colleges, which, as we have seen, include 11.7 percent Jews among their entering students. The low percentage for the invisible colleges is no doubt a hangover from the days when most were affiliated with a Protestant denomination or with the Roman Catholic Church; even though many of these have now become, in fact or in name, nonsectarian, the tendency for non-Christians not to enroll in these colleges remains. Past or current religious ties are evidenced also by the enrollment of Roman Catholic students. The percentages are virtually the same for the invisible and the community colleges (38.8 and 38.2, respectively), whereas the public four-year colleges enroll only 30.4 percent Roman Catholic students.

The differences among the three groups of colleges with respect to the percentages of students whose fathers have a postgraduate degree are worth noting: 10.6 for the invisible colleges, 6.3 for the state colleges, and 3.4 for the community colleges. (Again the elite colleges stand in sharp contrast: over one-third of their entering freshmen have fathers with a postgraduate degree.) Why do the invisible colleges attract a much larger proportion of these students than do the public colleges? One might surmise here that highly educated fathers have a bias in favor of private education.

Economic characteristics Turning to economic characteristics, we find that about one in five students entering the invisible colleges and community colleges comes from families with borderline poverty-level incomes (under $6,000); the figure for four-year public colleges is smaller (15.7 percent). Given these figures, one may conclude that the bias toward private education (or, perhaps, toward sectarian education) must indeed be strong, especially if parents with low incomes prefer to send their children to invisible colleges rather than to the state colleges, where expenses are considerably lower. Fewer students at public four-year and two-year colleges (18.2 percent and 12.7 percent, respectively) report that scholarship aid is a major source for financing their college educations, so students at the invisible colleges have the advantage there (28 percent being the comparative figure). On the other hand, invisible college students are more inclined to express "major concern" over finances (14 percent) than are students at the public colleges (about 1 in 10 of whom express such worries). This apparent contradiction is explained, of course, by the lower tuition and fees at public institutions.

High school background A larger proportion of the students entering public four-year and two-year colleges attended public high schools (about 88 percent in both cases) than did students entering invisible institutions (70.9 percent). With respect to their academic records, invisible college students and state college students are much alike: 11.6 percent of the former and 12.5 percent of the latter had high school grade averages of A. In sharp contrast, only 3 percent of the students entering community colleges had such a high average. A similar pattern occurs for class standing: 25.5 percent of the invisible college students, 22.6 percent of the state college students, but only 7.7 percent of the community college students reported having graduated in the upper tenth of their high school classes.

Degree plans Looking at degree plans, one is again struck by the similarity between students at invisible colleges and those at four-year public colleges. About 1 in 10 of both groups aspire to the Ph.D.; only 1 in 20 of the community college students have such high aspirations. Very few students in all three groups are interested in getting a medical or a law degree, and again the proportion is lowest among two-year public college students. As was pointed out previously, students entering the elite colleges have markedly higher degree aspirations.

Political preferences In the matter of political preferences, the students who call themselves "liberal" or "left" outnumber those who call themselves "moderately conservative" or "strongly conservative" in all three groups of institutions, though community college students seem more inclined to take a middle-of-the-road position. The numerical dominance of the liberals over conservatives, however, is not nearly so strong among these three groups as among students at elite colleges.

Career choices Table 30 compares the four groups of institutions (invisible, four-year public, two-year public, and elite) with respect to the career choices of their entering freshmen. It appears that the invisible colleges and the public four-year colleges have in common a substantial proportion of students who plan to become elementary and secondary school teachers; with the two-year public colleges, they share fairly large proportions of students seeking careers as nurses or health professionals (a category which excludes physicians and dentists). Inasmuch as the community colleges, with their two-year programs, cannot give the level of professional training in the health professions that is required for accreditation, these aspirations probably reflect long-term career plans that require eventual transfer to another institution.

The invisible colleges are strikingly similar to the community colleges and the state colleges in the relatively large proportions of their students who are inclined toward careers in business, a rather unpopular choice at elite colleges. Furthermore, at all three types of institutions, the occupations of physician, lawyer, and research scientist rank low in appeal. It is somewhat startling

TABLE 30   *Career choices of entering freshmen at four types of colleges*

	Mean percentage of entering freshmen			
Career	Invisible (N = 40)	Public 4-year (N = 21)	Public 2-year (N = 25)	Elite (N = 23)
Artist	6.9	5.6	4.8	8.4
Businessman	10.0	9.0	14.8	3.6
Clergyman	1.6	0.3	0.3	0.5
College teacher	1.5	1.3	0.7	3.9
Elementary teacher	14.7	16.9	6.9	1.6
Engineer	1.7	3.7	7.1	7.1
Farmer or forester	1.4	1.4	3.0	0.5
Health professional (non-M.D.)	5.1	3.9	4.7	1.1
Lawyer	2.7	2.9	1.2	8.0
Nurse	3.5	1.2	3.9	0.1
Physician (M.D.)	2.7	2.1	1.6	7.3
Research scientist	2.4	2.2	1.3	9.4
Secondary teacher	17.2	22.6	9.5	7.7
Other choice	18.1	15.7	30.5	18.5
Undecided	10.3	11.2	9.9	22.3

SOURCE: Creager, Astin, Boruch, Bayer, & Drew, 1969.

to find that the same percentage of community college students as elite college students (7.1) name engineer as their freshman career choice, whereas just over half as many state college students (3.7 percent) and even fewer invisible college students aspire to this career. The figures may be misleading, however, in that some question arises as to what the term *engineering* means to a particular respondent. The community colleges have many programs that train students in certain low-level technical aspects of what might broadly be called engineering; but it requires more than a two-year program to train full-fledged engineers with professional degrees. It is possible, of course, that these students plan to transfer to four-year colleges or universities to complete their professional training.

Community college students are roughly twice as likely as students at state colleges and invisible colleges to report career plans that fall into the "other choice" category in our list; these other choices are probably types of specialized technical occupations. All three groups, however, are more decided about their career plans (only about 1 in 10 says he is undecided) than are students at elite colleges (where the proportion is more than 1 in 5).

Overall, the career choice patterns of freshmen at invisible colleges come closest to those of state college students, particularly with respect to elementary and secondary teaching. The one exception is that four times as many invisible college students (1.6 percent) as state college students (0.3 percent) say that they plan to become clergymen, a difference easily explained by the religious affiliations of many invisible colleges. At some points, invisible college students come closer to being like community college students than state college students, specifically in their choices of the health professions and nursing. As was the case with engineering and the health professions, some question arises here about how particular respondents interpreted the term *nursing*. The community college student might, after two years of training, receive a degree as a practical nurse, but further training would be required for accreditation as a registered nurse. The patterns for all three groups of institutions are, with a few puzzling exceptions, almost diametrically opposed to the patterns for elite colleges.

SUMMARY In summary, it seems clear that students at the invisible colleges are substantially different from students at the elite colleges in their demographic characteristics, family backgrounds, high school achievements, and career choices. On the other hand, they are remarkably similar in many ways to freshmen at four-year public colleges, a finding that substantiates the contention that these two types of colleges compete with one another for students.

The implication here is that further expansion of the public colleges will seriously hurt the invisible colleges. Moreover, as programs in nursing and the health professions are further developed in the community colleges, the invisible colleges may find themselves in competition with this group of institutions as well.

5. *The Environment*

Objective measurement of the psychological "climate" or environment of collegiate institutions has become increasingly popular in educational research. Our analysis of the psychological characteristics of the environments of invisible colleges is based on extensive data collected from an objective environmental inventory. Participants in the inventory were drawn from a sample of 246 colleges and universities (Astin, 1971*b*). The data included 33 factors from the Inventory of College Activities (ICA) (Astin, 1968*b*).

The ICA consists of 33 scales. Twenty-seven of these are measures of the college environment, and eight are measures of the colleges "image" similar to the scales of the *College Characteristics Index* (Pace & Stern, 1958) and the *College and University Environmental Scales* (Pace, 1963). The 27 "stimulus" measures are based on the frequency of occurrence of various types of environmental "stimuli." A *stimulus* is defined as any behavior, event, or other institutional characteristic which is potentially capable of changing the student's sensory input and the existence or occurrence of which can be confirmed by independent observation. Some examples are the percentage of students who have blind dates, the average number of hours per week students spend studying, the amount of class discussion permitted by the professors, and the frequency of various types of examinations. The 25 measures of environmental stimuli are divided into three categories: the peer environment (interpersonal and noninterpersonal), the classroom environment, and the administrative environment. The eight college "image" factors are based on the students' subjective judgments about such matters as the degree of concern shown for students by the administration, the emphasis on social life, and the snobbishness and sophistication of the college. (For a list and brief description of each of these 33 measures, see Appendix B.)

From the 246 institutions that participated in the original ICA normative study, we identified 35 invisible colleges and 20 elite colleges for which we had complete data on all 33 ICA measures. The mean score for the 35 invisible colleges on each of the 33 ICA factors is indicated by the solid line in Figure 3; the broken line shows the mean environmental profile for the total sample of four-year institutions ($N = 161$). The scales for percentiles and T scores, which are shown on the vertical axis of Figure 3, correspond to national norms for all institutions ($N = 246$).

Perhaps the most noteworthy aspect of Figure 3 is that the environmental characteristics of the typical invisible college are in many ways like those of four-year colleges in general. (To some extent, this similarity is misleading, since invisible colleges constitute a large segment of the total population of four-year colleges.) Nevertheless, certain differences between the invisible colleges and all four-year colleges should be pointed out. Students attending invisible colleges, for example, are more likely to come into conflict with regulations (ICA factor 13) than are students in all four-year colleges, a finding consistent with the relative severity of administrative policies concerning drinking, aggression, and sexual behavior (factors 22, 23, and 24) at these institutions. Moving to the college image factors, we find that students attending invisible colleges tend more to feel that their college shows concern for their individual welfare (factor 27) than do students attending other types of four-year colleges.

The ICA environmental profile for the 20 elite colleges is shown in Figure 4. The discrepancies here between the mean scores for elite colleges and those for all four-year colleges are much larger than was the case for invisible institutions. In fact, if we compare the profiles of invisible and elite colleges (the solid lines of Figures 3 and 4, respectively), we find highly significant differences ($p < .01$) on nearly two-thirds of the environmental measures. The major environmental differences can be summarized as follows:

The peer environment   Students attending invisible colleges seem to be much less independent (factor 3) than students attending elite colleges, *independence* being defined here as the tendency to be contentious and argumentative and to participate in demonstrations against administrative policies. Elite college students are much more likely to indulge in social drinking and, by the same token, to engage in few formal religious activities, such as attending church, saying grace, or reading the Bible regularly. (The factor

FIGURE 3 *Mean scores of invisible colleges and of four-year colleges in general on inventory of college activities factors*

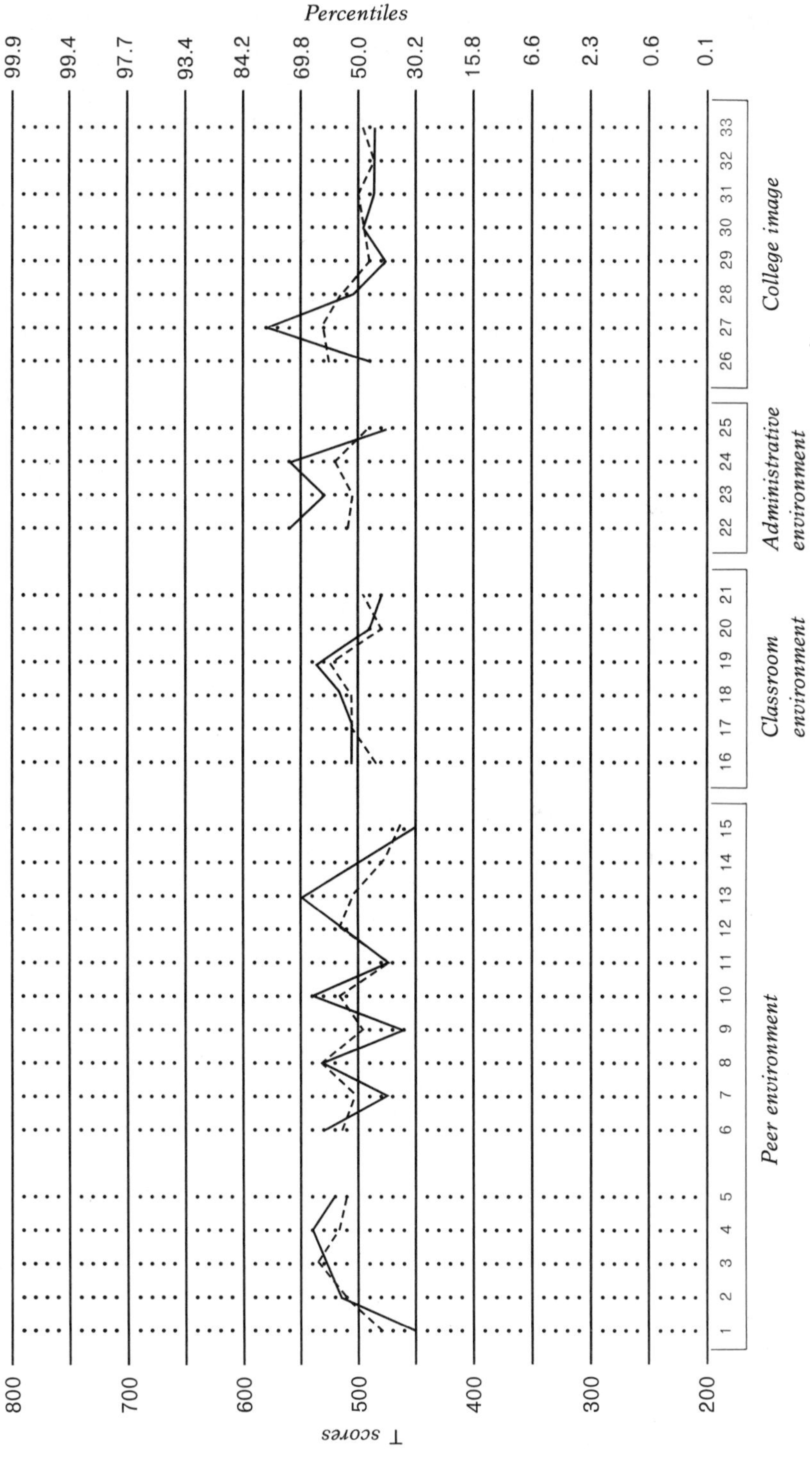

Mean scores for invisible colleges (*N* = 35)
Mean scores for all four-year colleges (*N* = 161)

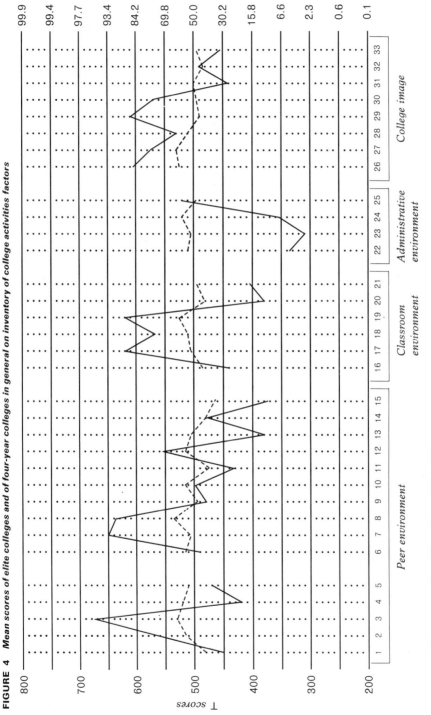

FIGURE 4 *Mean scores of elite colleges and of four-year colleges in general on inventory of college activities factors*

involved here—factor 7—is bipolar; for a fuller description, see Appendix B.) They are also more musically and artistically inclined, both as performers and as observers (factor 8). Invisible college students, on the other hand, are friendlier with one another and place a higher value on getting along with other people (factor 4). They have informal dates more frequently (factor 5) and are more apt to drive cars during the school year (factor 15). As was the case in the comparisons involving invisible colleges and four-year colleges in general, the invisible college student is more likely to come into conflict with college regulations (factor 13) than is the elite college student. (As we shall see in discussing the administrative environments of these two types of institutions, this tendency is probably attributable to the severity of administrative policies against certain types of behavior.) It seems likely that these differences in peer environments are in part the result of the differences (noted in Chapter 4) in the characteristics of students at invisible and at elite colleges.

The classroom environment   Although the classroom environment of the typical invisible college is much the same as that of four-year colleges in general (see Figure 3), it differs considerably from that of the typical elite college. In the classroom of the typical invisible college, the student is much less verbally aggressive (factor 17); the instructor is less likely to be an extrovert who projects enthusiasm and humor (factor 18); he is also less apt to be on familiar terms with his students (factor 19). In addition, grading practices are more severe; students are much more likely to fail a course during the freshman year and to get lower average grades (factor 21). The most striking difference between the classroom environments of the invisible and the elite colleges lies in the degree of organization in the classroom (factor 20). The classes at invisible colleges are much more highly structured: the instructors usually take attendance, assign seats to students, and hold classes at a regularly scheduled time and place; students are rarely late to class. The classroom environment of the elite colleges seems much more informal and relaxed in these matters.

The administrative environment   It is in the severity of their administrative policies toward certain types of behavior that the invisible colleges differ most dramatically from the elite colleges. The invisible colleges are far more likely to act in loco parentis, inflicting harsher penalties (e.g., suspension or expulsion) for drinking (factor 22); for aggression, particularly as expressed in demonstrations against administrative policies, but also for that expressed in such minor misbehavior as dormitory raids and water fights (factor 23); and for heterosexual activity, as defined by regulations against a student's being alone in his or her room with a date (the rules seem to be applied more strictly to women) or coming in late from a date (factor 24). Most elite colleges have much more lenient policies in these three areas. With respect to administrative policies against cheating (factor 25), elite colleges tend to be slightly more strict, but the difference between the two types of institutions is not very great.

The college image   Students attending elite and invisible colleges differ considerably in their impressions of the college environment. Specifically, students attending elite colleges are more likely to see their environment as permissive (factor 29); academically competitive, with respect both to perceived pressure for high grades and to perceived high academic ability of their fellow students (factor 26); and snobbish (factor 30). Students attending invisible colleges, on the other hand, are somewhat more likely to feel that both athletics (factor 31) and social activities (factor 33) are heavily emphasized, perhaps too much so.

THE INVISIBLE COLLEGE AND THE PUBLIC FOUR-YEAR COLLEGE   Since the public four-year college is probably the chief competitor for students who are potential entrants to the invisible colleges, the question of how the environments of these two types of colleges compare is a significant one. From our sample of 246 institutions, we identified 22 public colleges (8 teachers colleges and 14 liberal arts colleges, many of which were formerly teachers colleges). The mean ICA profile for these 22 colleges is shown in Figure 5.

The peer environment   In general, the peer environments of invisible colleges and public colleges are very similar; their close resemblance is not surprising in view of the earlier finding (Chapter 4) that these two types of institutions enroll students who are alike in many ways. They differ in that students at the typical invisible college are more likely to be indecisive about their career choice (factor 10) and to come into conflict with regulations more frequently (factor 13), whereas students at the typical public four-year college are more likely to drive cars during the college year (factor 15). The greater certainty that the public college students

FIGURE 5 *Mean scores of invisible colleges and of public four-year colleges on inventory of college activities factors*

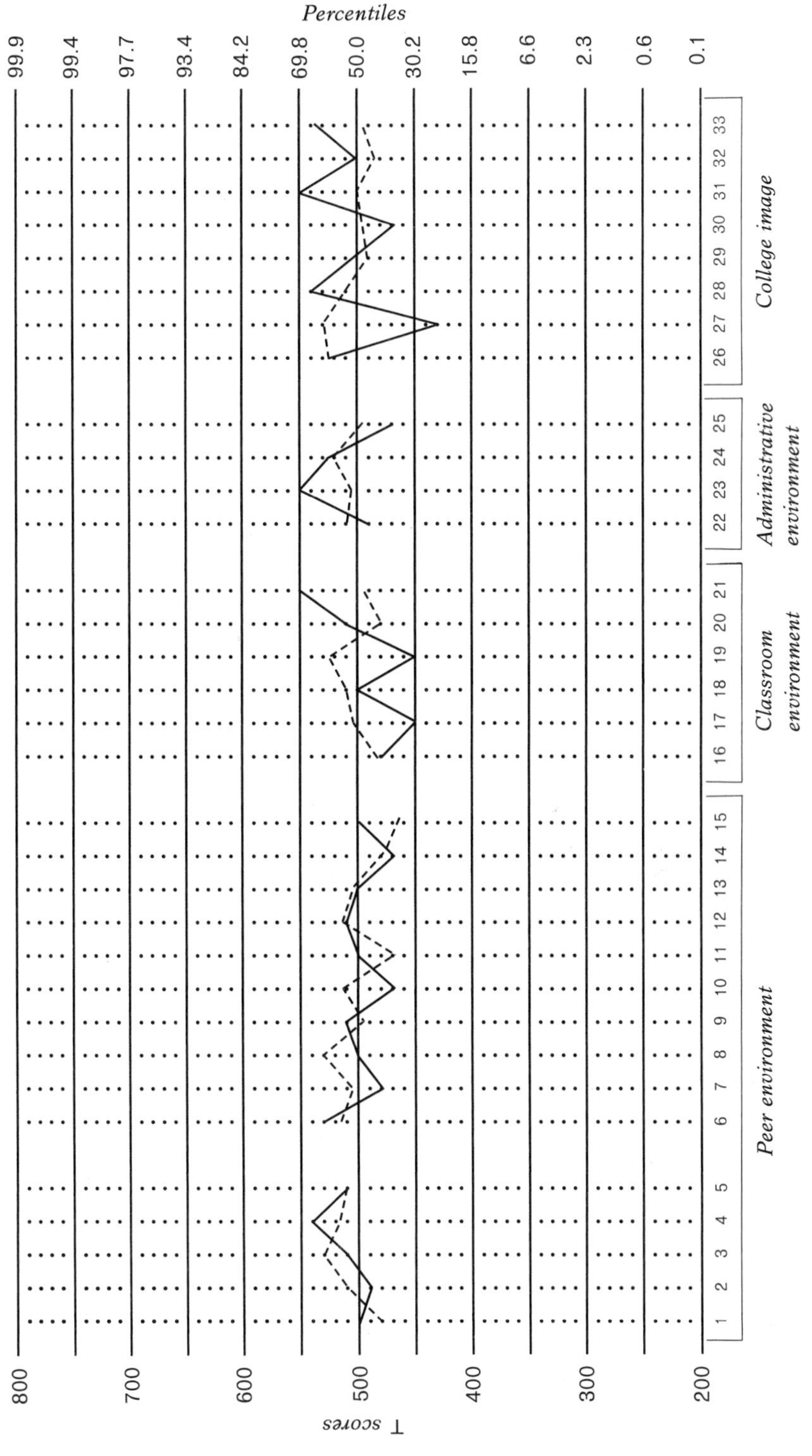

—— Mean scores for invisible colleges ($N = 35$)
------- Mean scores for public four-year colleges ($N = 22$)

manifest about their career plans may be attributable to their relatively high concentration in vocationally oriented courses; their greater use of cars is probably explained by the large proportion of commuters who attend these colleges. The inclusion of Roman Catholic institutions in the sample of invisible colleges probably accounts for the greater frequency with which students are penalized for infractions of college regulations.

The classroom environment   The most striking difference between the classroom environments of public colleges and invisible colleges is in familiarity with the instructor (factor 19); the invisible colleges score more than three-fourths of a standard deviation above the public colleges on this measure, which is defined chiefly by the warmth of the relationship and extent of personal contact between instructor and student. Students at the typical public college are also less outspoken and argumentative in class (factor 17). Both these differences are probably attributable to the larger size of the public colleges. The two types of institutions differ also in severity of grading (factor 21); students at public colleges are more likely to receive low or failing grades.

The administrative environment   Administrative policies concerning aggression (factor 23), sexual conduct (factor 24), and cheating (factor 25) are similar in the public and the invisible colleges. The typical public college, however, is much more permissive about drinking than is the typical invisible college.

The college image   By far the greatest environmental difference between public and invisible colleges lies in the students' impressions of the friendliness and warmth of the institution, its concern for the individual student (factor 27). The invisible colleges score fully 1½ standard deviations above the public colleges on this measure. Again, it seems likely that the larger size of the public colleges is the major reason for this difference in the student's image of his institution. (On this factor, invisible colleges are more akin to elite colleges, where students also feel that the college is concerned about them as human beings.) In addition, students at public colleges are more likely than are students at invisible colleges to have the impression that athletics and social life are greatly emphasized.

ENVIRON-
MENTAL
PROFILES OF
DIFFERENT
TYPES OF
INVISIBLE
COLLEGES Are the invisible colleges homogeneous with respect to environmental characteristics, or do they fall into distinct subgroups, each with its own special characteristics? To explore this question, we divided our sample of 35 invisible colleges into three categories: private nonsectarian ($N=9$), Protestant ($N=14$), and Roman Catholic ($N=12$). (There were two few Protestant institutions to obtain reliable profiles for separate denominations.) Their environmental profiles have been plotted in Figure 6. Although most of the differences are not as great as those found for invisible and elite colleges, several are substantial enough to warrant comment.

The peer environment The largest difference in the peer environments of the three subgroups occurs on the factor of conflict with regulations (factor 13), where the Roman Catholic institutions score more than 2 standard deviations above the nonsectarian institutions and about $1\frac{1}{2}$ standard deviations above the Protestant institutions. Catholic colleges have a much more feminine environment (factor 6) than do the other two types of invisible colleges, mostly because they include many women's colleges.

At nonsectarian institutions, the sleeping habits of students are markedly irregular (factor 11), even more so than is true at elite colleges. These students — who usually live away from home — often stay up all night, take pills to stay awake, oversleep and miss classes, and take naps during the day. In addition, they manifest much more independence (factor 3) than do students at Roman Catholic colleges, though the difference on this measure between nonsectarian institutions and Protestant ones is not so marked.

Students at Protestant institutions have fewer informal dates (factor 5), drink less and engage in religious activities more (factor 7), and indulge less in such leisure activities as going to movies and playing games (factor 9).

The classroom environment Differences in the classroom environments of the three types of invisible colleges are generally consistent with the stereotypes of the three groups. On verbal aggressiveness (factor 17), for example, the nonsectarian institutions score highest, the Protestant institutions lowest, and the Catholic institutions in between. Students at Protestant institutions are most likely to be on friendly terms with the instructor (factor

FIGURE 6 *Mean scores of the three types of invisible colleges (nonsectarian, Protestant, and Roman Catholic) on inventory of college activities factors*

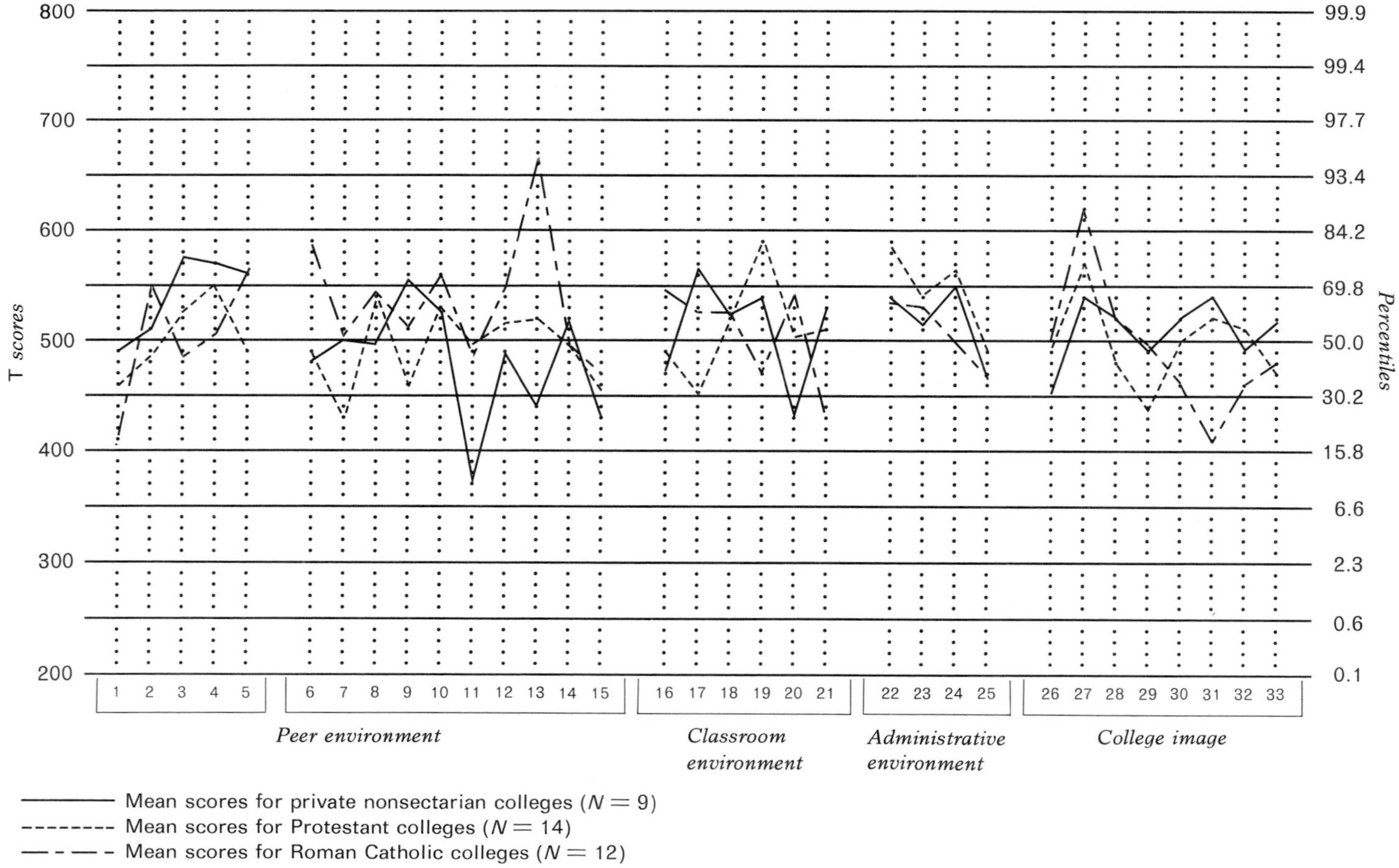

Mean scores for private nonsectarian colleges ($N = 9$)
Mean scores for Protestant colleges ($N = 14$)
Mean scores for Roman Catholic colleges ($N = 12$)

19), those at Catholic institutions are least likely, and nonsectarian institutions occupy a middle position on this measure. Still a third pattern is revealed with respect to organization in the classroom (factor 20): Catholic institutions have the most highly structured and formal classes, nonsectarian institutions the least structured, and Protestant institutions fall between the two extremes. The classroom environments of Roman Catholic institutions have two other distinctive characteristics. Their students and instructors show a greater interest and a deeper involvement in the class (factor 16), and grading standards tend to be lenient; few freshmen receive failing grades (factor 21).

The administrative environment   The patterns for all three types of invisible colleges on the administrative factors are strikingly similar, although some differences are worth noting. Policies against drinking (factor 22) are most severe at Protestant institutions and about equally severe at Catholic and nonsectarian ones. Both Protestant and nonsectarian colleges have fairly severe policies against sex (factor 24), whereas, in this instance, Catholic institutions seem to be somewhat more lenient. Aggressive behavior and cheating (factors 23 and 25) are penalized to about the same extent at all three types of invisible colleges.

The college image   Students at Catholic institutions and at nonsectarian institutions differ most widely in their impressions of their colleges. The former tend to see the institution as manifesting much greater concern for the individual student (factor 27); the latter are much more inclined to feel that their institution overemphasizes athletics (factor 31). The only distinctive feature of the college image at Protestant institutions is that their students have a greater tendency to feel that the college is restrictive rather than permissive (factor 29).

In summary, the invisible colleges are not a homogeneous group with respect to their environmental attributes. To be sure, certain aspects of their environments (severity of administrative policies against certain student behaviors, for example) tend to be highly similar. But there are some striking differences as well. In general, the Roman Catholic colleges and the nonsectarian ones stand at opposite poles, with the Protestant institutions occupying a middle position.

DISCUSSION Our analysis of the three subgroups of invisible colleges failed to reveal any one that resembled elite colleges more closely than did the other two. This failure is somewhat surprising. For example, one might hypothesize that, compared with the other two subgroups, the nonsectarian group has environmental attributes more closely resembling those in our sample of elite colleges, all but one of which are nonsectarian. Even though there were some similarities—in students' tendencies to be more independent (factor 3) and verbally aggressive (factor 17); to have irregular sleeping habits (factor 11); and to come into conflict with regulations only infrequently (factor 13); and in the relative lack of organization in the classroom (factor 20)—the nonsectarian colleges differ considerably from the elite colleges (in some cases even more so than did one or both of the other two subgroups of invisible colleges) on certain other measures. For instance, the students at the nonsectarian colleges are less inclined to drink (and more inclined to engage in religious behavior), less involved in musical and artistic activities, and less inclined to have personal contacts with their instructors than are students at elite colleges. In addition, grading standards are more strict at the nonsectarian invisible colleges. With respect to administrative policies, the elite colleges are much more inclined to be lenient, especially with respect to student aggression (although on this item, the nonsectarian invisible colleges are slightly less severe than the other two subgroups). Finally, with respect to college image, the elite college student is far more likely to see his institution as academically competitive and as permissive than is the nonsectarian invisible college student. In short, it is not possible to order the three subgroups of invisible colleges on a continuum of similarity to the elite college, even though they differ from one another substantially on several environmental attributes.

Although the invisible colleges are in many ways more like the public colleges than the elite private colleges, they are also different in certain potentially important respects: students at the public colleges have much less personal contact with their instructors (factor 19) and are much more inclined to feel that the institution is impersonal and cold (factor 27). Our analyses of the three subgroups of invisible colleges failed to reveal any particular subgroup that resembles the public colleges more closely than do the other two.

SUMMARY Our analyses of 33 measures of the peer, classroom, and administrative environments, and of the college image, make it clear that the invisible colleges are not a homogeneous group of institutions. Rather, they encompass a great diversity and range of environmental characteristics. Considered as a group, however, they differ from the elite colleges in many ways. These differences are no doubt attributable chiefly to differences in student inputs.

Similar comparisons between invisible colleges and public colleges revealed far fewer differences, probably because the students entering public colleges are very like those entering invisible colleges (see Chapter 4). The largest differences—which involve concern for the individual student (factor 27) and familiarity with the instructor (factor 19)—are almost certainly attributable to the public college's larger size.

The major finding here—that, with respect to their student inputs and their environments, invisible colleges are much more similar to public colleges than to elite colleges—has important policy implications. To illustrate, most legislators, whether federal or state, tend to regard "the small college" or the "private college" as a homogeneous category, separate and distinct from the large public college. Yet the invisible college and the elite college—except for their being privately controlled and rather small—have very little in common. They serve radically different student clienteles, and their social and intellectual environments are highly dissimilar. By the same token, the public college, except for its larger size, closely resembles the invisible college both in its environmental characteristics and in the students that it attempts to serve. These facts suggest that, in long-range planning on a statewide or national basis, elite and invisible private colleges should be clearly distinguished from one another and that every effort should be made to avoid unnecessary duplication of functions and programs in the public four-year and the invisible private colleges.

6. The Impact of Invisible Colleges on Their Students

For the prospective student, attending college may have two basically different sorts of consequences. The first involves the effects of the college on the student's personal and intellectual development. These consequences, which may be labeled *educational effects,* include the student's experiences during his undergraduate years, his intellectual growth and development, and the quality of his vocational preparation. It includes, as well, any changes in his values, attitudes, interests, habits, mental health, and so forth, that are attributable to the college experience. What we are concerned with here are the educational effects that derive from a college's relative visibility or invisibility.

The second category of consequences may be referred to as the *fringe benefits* of attending a given college. By this term, we mean any outcome that results not from an actual change in the student himself but rather from his having done his time, so to speak, at a particular college and from the knowledge that other people have of this fact and the inferences they draw from it. The student who has a baccalaureate degree from a prestigious college may well find that it gives him certain vocational and social advantages quite out of proportion to his capabilities. In fact, many graduate and professional schools, as well as many employers, consider the applicant's undergraduate institution of prime importance in evaluating his qualifications. In short, an undergraduate degree from one institution may constitute a much better entrée to a graduate or professional school or to a high-level job than does the same degree from another institution, regardless of the candidate's real talent and regardless of what he has learned or what skills he has acquired in college. It seems safe to assume that the more visible an institution, the greater and more numerous are these fringe benefits.

But what of the first sort of consequence: the educational effects of visibility or invisibility? In what ways do an institution's small size and low selectivity influence the student's learning and personal development? During recent years, increasing effort has been devoted to assessing the effects of institutional characteristics, including selectivity and size, on the student. Although the findings cannot be regarded as definitive, since much of the research is still in progress, enough evidence has accumulated to permit us to make certain tentative conclusions about the educational impact of institutional visibility on the student.

First, with respect to selectivity, the common belief that an elite or "high-quality" institution provides a superior environment for learning is so far not supported by the evidence (Astin, 1968*b*; Nichols, 1964; Rock, Centra, & Linn, 1970). On the contrary, the cognitive skills of a student seem to develop at the same rate whatever the selectivity of the institution he attends. Thus, contrary to popular opinion, the superior student is apparently no better off attending a highly selective institution; he would develop just as well intellectually if he attended a less selective one. Conversely, the few average or below-average students who manage to get into highly selective colleges do not seem to become unduly intimidated or discouraged, and their dropout rate is in fact only slightly greater than that of the typical bright student at such institutions (Astin, 1970*d*). Although the studies cited cannot be regarded as the final word on the effects of selectivity on intellectual achievement, they do suggest that our traditional definitions of institutional "quality" may be inadequate and even erroneous.

It comes as no surprise that selectivity has a negative effect on the student's grades (Astin, 1971*c*; Astin, 1970*a*). That is, a given student will tend to get lower grades at a selective college than at an unselective one. In spite of his lower grades, however, he is less likely to drop out of a selective college than an unselective one. This finding holds true for the less able student as well as for the bright one (Astin, 1971*c*).

With respect to an institution's size, recent research (as reported in the previous chapter) seems to confirm the folklore about the "small intimate college" as opposed to the "impersonal multiversity." In the small college, faculty and students are usually on fairly familiar terms, and both tend to be interested and absorbed in the classwork. The environment is cohesive, and the students feel that the administration is concerned about them as individuals. (These findings apply equally to small invisible and small elite colleges.) The environment of the very large institution, on the other hand, tends to be cold and competitive. Faculty and students are not deeply involved in the activities of the classroom and have relatively few contacts with each other outside of it. Moreover, the students at big institutions often feel that the administration is rather indifferent to their welfare (Astin, 1968a).

What effects does size have on a student's academic progress and intellectual development? One recent study (Astin & Panos, 1969) indicates that attending a small institution increases the student's chances of staying in college and of raising his educational aspirations (in that he becomes more inclined to get an advanced degree). In contrast, the large institution has a negative impact on the student's desire to pursue graduate training and to get the Ph.D., although it slightly increases his desire to get a professional degree. Consistent with this pattern, he becomes more inclined to change his career choice to businessman or lawyer and less inclined to become a teacher (elementary, secondary, or college) or a natural scientist. These findings run directly counter to the common assumption that the large university, with its well-equipped laboratories and distinguished research scientists, provides the ideal environment for encouraging the student's interest in graduate training, research, and college teaching.

Another point revealed by recent research (Astin & Bayer, 1971; Bayer & Astin, 1969; Peterson, 1968) is that the larger institutions are more likely than are the smaller ones to experience major incidents of campus unrest, particularly of the kind that involves physical violence.

Finally, attending a large institution often leads to a diminution in the student's concept of his popularity and his academic ability (Nichols, 1967). Although any explanation must at this point be tentative, these environmental effects are probably attributable in part to the apparent coldness, indifference, and impersonality that characterize most large institutions. Size does not, however, affect the student's cognitive development in any discernible way (Astin, 1968b).

EFFECTS OF INVISIBILITY   So far, we have considered the independent effects of size and selectivity, not their combined effects or the effects of invisibility per se. Since the studies cited above do not deal with size and selectivity in combination, we cannot extract the invisible colleges for separate study.

Fortunately, however, a more recent large-scale study of institutional impact on students (Astin, 1971a) provides us with an opportunity to look at invisible colleges as a group and in broad perspective. Although the results of this ongoing study are far from complete, the preliminary findings provide some valuable insights.

Briefly, the study involves longitudinal analyses of data on students attending a national sample of some 300 colleges of all types (Astin, Panos, & Creager, 1966). We are now in the midst of examining four-year longitudinal data, but the only results available at this writing come from a one-year longitudinal analysis of students who entered college in the fall of 1967 and were followed up one year later, during the summer of 1968. The follow-up questionnaire repeated many of the items that were on the original questionnaire. In addition, data on dropout status and freshman grade-point average (GPA) were obtained directly from the institutions, which also supplied us with scores on aptitude tests that the students had taken during their junior and senior years in high school.

The basic design of these analyses was as follows. First, student input (meaning the characteristics of entering freshmen, including their high school aptitude test scores) was partialed out from the students' responses to the follow-up questionnaire items and also from the other information provided by the institutions. Thus each follow-up questionnaire item, plus dropout status and GPA, became the criterion measures. All student input variables that contributed significantly ($p < .05$) to the prediction of each criterion measure were first controlled by means of multiple regression analyses (which, in effect, equate students statistically in terms of their entering characteristics). Next, we examined the effects of a wide variety of institutional characteristics, including institutional invisibility. In all, our sample contained 28,000 students attending 186 different institutions. Among these were 2,667 students attending a total of 22 invisible colleges.

To analyze the impact of the invisible colleges, we first computed a mean *expected* score on each criterion measure, using as our basis the regression equations mentioned above. Then, from responses to the follow-up survey, we obtained the mean *actual* score. If the mean expected score and the mean actual score do not differ significantly, one may conclude that the impact of the invisible college on a particular criterion is nil. If the mean actual score exceeds the mean expected score, then one may conclude that the invisible college has a positive effect on the particular outcome in question. Conversely, if the mean actual score is significantly lower than the mean expected score, then one may conclude that the invisible college has a negative effect on the outcome. In short, we can see to what extent and in what directions the students at invisible colleges are affected by their institutions, in comparison with college students in general.[1]

As was pointed out before, it is the public four-year college that poses the greatest threat to the invisible college in the competition for students, faculty, and funds. Moreover, in planning for the support of higher education at the state and national levels, it seems reasonable to regard the public college as the principal administrative alternative to the invisible college. For these reasons, we chose as a comparison group the 2,321 students at the 18 public colleges in our sample and went through the same process of computing mean expected and mean actual scores and examining the differences.

Of the 51 criterion measures, 25 were significantly affected by attendance at either an invisible or a public four-year college. The students' mean actual performance on the criterion measure differed significantly from their mean expected performance (that is, from what was predicted on the basis of their freshman input characteristics) in at least one of these types of colleges. Table 31, which lists the 25 variables, also indicates the direction of the effect: positive, negative, or not significant (n.s.).

It is clear that the two groups of institutions tend to affect their students in contrasting ways. Of the 25 items shown in Table 31, the invisible colleges and the public colleges have a similar effect, and that negative, on only 1 item: "Saw a foreign movie." The comparative effects of the two types of institutions are significantly different on 19 of the 24 remaining items. On four of these, the two groups have significant effects in opposite directions.

Effects on staying in college and on GPA   The first two items, which have to do with the student's returning to or leaving the

---

[1] For a fuller description of methodological problems, see Astin, (1970*b*).

college of matriculation, reveal an interesting difference between invisible and public colleges. The latter seem to have a greater holding power over their students (insofar as the students are more likely to return after the first year) than do other types of colleges, including the invisible ones. But it does not follow that students at invisible colleges are more likely to leave higher education altogether than are students at public colleges. On the contrary, the invisible colleges have a significant positive effect on the student's enrolling in some other institution for the sophomore year, whereas students at public colleges, if they do not return to the college of matriculation, are not likely to enroll anywhere else for their sophomore year. In short, any conclusions about the comparative attrition rates of the two types of colleges depend on how one defines the term *dropout.* (It should be remembered that these findings are based on a one-year follow-up; very possibly, the public college student who drops out may do so for only a short period of time. The point is that many do not enroll immediately in another institution.)

The third item in Table 31, the student's academic performance during the freshman year, indicates that students at public four-year colleges receive grades consistent with their past performance in high school, whereas students at invisible colleges receive grades that are significantly higher than would be expected from the data on their characteristics as entering freshmen. Recent research on the institutional characteristics affecting academic performance (Astin, 1971c) suggests that this effect is primarily attributable to the low selectivity of the invisible colleges. In short, the invisible colleges have somewhat easier grading standards than do the public colleges.

Effects on satisfaction with college   The fourth item in Table 31, which was included in the one-year follow-up questionnaire, asked the student to rate his reactions to the college on a five-point scale: very satisfied, satisfied, on the fence, dissatisfied, and very dissatisfied. Although most students in all types of institutions, including public colleges, tend to express overall satisfaction, students attending invisible colleges deviate from this general pattern. It seems safe to conclude that the student who attends an invisible college is likely to be somewhat less satisfied with his college after one year than is the student attending a public college.

Since this measure was a global assessment that did not attempt to isolate specific aspects of the institution that students found

TABLE 31 *Effects of 22 invisible colleges and 18 public four-year colleges on selected student outcomes during the freshman year*

	Effects on criterion measures of	
Criterion measure	Invisible colleges	Public 4-yr. colleges
Academic progress		
1–Returned to same college after one year	n.s.*	positive
2–Enrolled in any college after one year	positive	n.s.
3–Freshman GPA	positive	n.s.
Satisfaction		
4–Satisfaction with freshman year	negative	n.s.
Behaviors and activities		
5–Was a guest in a professor's home	positive	negative
6–Argued with a teacher in class	positive	n.s.
7–Asked a teacher for advice after class	n.s.	negative
8–Slept or dozed in class	n.s.	negative
9–Typed a homework assignment	positive	n.s.
10–Did extra reading for a course	positive	n.s.
11–Tutored another student	positive	n.s.
12–Discussed religion with other students	positive	negative
13–Discussed sports with other students	positive	n.s.
14–Participated in demonstrations on racial issues	positive	negative
15–Participated in demonstrations against administrative policies	n.s.	positive
16–Took a trip of more than 500 miles	positive	negative
17–Got a traffic ticket	negative	n.s.
18–Played chess	n.s.	positive
19–Visited an art gallery or museum	negative	n.s.
20–Saw a foreign movie	negative	negative
Attitudes and values		
21–Realistically, an individual person can do little to bring about changes in our society	n.s.	positive
22–Colleges would be improved if organized sports were de-emphasized	negative	n.s.
23–Most college officials have been too lax in dealing with student protests on campus	n.s.	negative
24–Women should be subject to the draft	n.s.	negative
25–The voting age should be lowered to 18	n.s.	negative

*n.s. = nonsignificant ($p > .05$).

satisfactory or unsatisfactory, it may be useful here to mention some other findings connected with this outcome. By far the greatest degree of dissatisfaction (again measured by discrepancies between predicted and actual satisfaction) is registered by students at technological institutions. Actual satisfaction exceeds expected satisfaction most in public and private universities. An examination of the specific institutional characteristics that affect overall satisfaction suggests that the invisible college's negative impact is primarily attributable to two factors: their relatively restrictive policies on student conduct (drinking, in particular) and the presence of several women's colleges in the sample. (Students at women's colleges, regardless of the institution's visibility, tend to express less satisfaction with college than do students at coeducational or men's colleges.) Other institutional characteristics contributing to dissatisfaction include the relatively poor school spirit at the invisible colleges (see Chapter 4), their location (primarily in the South and Midwest), their lack of affluence, and, paradoxically, their low tuition fees.

Effects on behavior and activities   Sixteen of the behavioral items in the follow-up questionnaire were significantly affected by one or both of the two groups of colleges. Perhaps the most striking difference occurs on items having to do with personal contacts between faculty and students. Attendance at an invisible college seems to increase the chances that a student will be a guest in a professor's home or will argue with a teacher in class. By contrast, attendance at a public college makes it less likely that the student will be a guest in a professor's home or that he will ask a teacher for advice after class. The pattern here is clear: relations between students and faculty are more open and friendly at invisible colleges than at public colleges; the larger size of the public colleges is no doubt the major factor here.

Invisible colleges seem also to foster behavior that indicates increased motivation for academic work, e.g., typing homework assignments and doing extra reading for class. Public colleges have no particular effect on either of these two behaviors.

Yet another area where invisible colleges have a positive effect and public colleges either no effect or a negative one is that of increased student interaction. Students at invisible colleges are likely, beyond expectation, to tutor other students, to discuss sports together, and to discuss religion together. Public colleges have no significant effects on the first two items and a negative effect on the last, which may in part reflect the greater commitment that many invisible colleges have to formal religion.

One of the most interesting contrasts between invisible and public colleges concerns participation in demonstrations. A student is more likely to engage in demonstrations over racial issues if he attends an invisible college and less likely to participate in such demonstrations if he attends a public college. Conversely, a student is more likely to protest against administrative policies if he attends a public college, whereas this likelihood is unaffected by his attending an invisible college.

Attendance at an invisible college makes it more likely that the student will take a trip of over 500 miles but less likely that he will get a traffic ticket. The effect of attendance at a public college on the student's likelihood of taking so long a trip is just the opposite, although his chances of getting a traffic ticket are about what one would expect. These findings are consistent with the greater amount of commuting done by the public college students (see Chapter 4) and with the residential status of the invisible college student, which would tend to increase his chances of taking a long trip (presumably to his home).

The three other behavioral outcomes listed in Table 31 fall into no discernible pattern, so they will simply be mentioned in passing. The student who attends a public college is less likely to sleep or doze in class than would be expected; invisible colleges do not seem to affect this activity (or, rather, inactivity). The public college has a positive effect on playing chess; the invisible college has a negative effect on visiting an art gallery or museum. No easy interpretation suggests itself for any of these differences.

Effects on attitudes and values   Turning to the last five items in Table 31, which have to do with attitudes and values, we find that the invisible colleges have an impact on only one: their students grow less apt to feel that colleges would be improved if organized sports were not so heavily emphasized. Public colleges, on the other hand, have several significant effects on attitudes, although no consistent pattern is apparent. For example, they seem to strengthen students' pessimism about the ability of the individual to change society. (Perhaps this finding reflects the feelings of anonymity and depersonalization that frequently result from attending such colleges; see the previous chapter.) Furthermore, during their freshman year students at public colleges grow more likely to disagree with the viewpoint that college officials are too lenient toward student protesters (a shift in a seemingly liberal or left direction). At the same time, they come to disagree more with the idea that women should be drafted and that the voting age should be lowered to 18 (an apparent shift to the right).

Effects on career choice   One other aspect of the effects of invisible colleges (not shown in Table 31) deserves mention. In an earlier study (Astin & Panos, 1969), a national sample of students who had matriculated in the fall of 1961, at which time they completed the freshman questionnaire, were followed up in the summer of 1965, when presumably they would have graduated from college. For purposes of the present report, we separated from the total sample the invisible colleges and the elite colleges and examined their comparative effects on three outcomes: (a) educational attainment (completion of four years of undergraduate work; attainment of the baccalaureate), (b) educational aspirations (highest degree sought), and (c) final major field and career choice. Two points should be noted here. First, this analysis deals with longer-range effects than those we have been discussing heretofore (over a four-year period rather than just over the freshman year). Second, the comparison here is not between invisible and public colleges but between invisible colleges and elite colleges.

These two groups of colleges have no differential impact on the student's educational attainment or his degree plans. They do, however, have differential effects on his final major and career plans. Elite colleges tend to steer their students toward majors and career choices in the arts, humanities, and social sciences, whereas the invisible colleges steer their students toward the physical sciences (physics, chemistry, the earth sciences, and so forth), the health professions (non-M.D.), and, to a lesser extent, the biological sciences.

SUMMARY   Obviously, given the complexity and diversity of the higher educational system in the United States, the rising costs of education, and the growing need for coordination and long-range planning, it is essential that public policy be based on sound and complete information rather than on folklore. In particular, educational decision makers should be aware of the impact of different types of colleges on the student. Yet, as we have seen, one whole segment of the institutional population —a segment that encompasses about 500 institutions and about 500,000 students—has been virtually ignored in the literature of higher education. The focus has been chiefly on that group of institutions which, because of their size and selectivity, are highly visible. But, according to our analyses, these two defining attributes turn out to have somewhat different effects from those commonly supposed by professional educators and the lay public alike.

For example, there seems to be no special "value added" by attending a highly selective "center of excellence," a finding that directly controverts the folklore. Research into the effects of institutional size, on the other hand, generally confirms popular belief about large institutions: their students seem to feel more depersonalized and more alienated, and consequently they often lose their motivation to get an advanced degree and even leave college entirely, perhaps never to return.

The pattern of effects that the invisible colleges have on the student's personal development contrasts markedly with the pattern for public four-year colleges. The freshman enrolling at a public college may be more likely to return there for the sophomore year; but, on the other hand, the student who drops out of the invisible college at the end of his freshman year is more likely to enroll in some other institution immediately.

Consistent with this difference is the finding that invisible colleges fare less well than do public colleges in the matter of the student's overall satisfaction with his freshman-year experience. The relatively low rating that students give the invisible colleges is probably the result of the rather strict parietal rules of these institutions.

With respect to behavior, the invisible colleges are much more likely than are the public colleges to provide opportunities for personal interactions between faculty and students and among students. This pattern of differences is probably attributable to the smaller size of the invisible colleges, which in general, however, have little effect on the attitudes of their students. In the matter of career choice four years after matriculation, invisible colleges have a positive effect on students' plans to become physical scientists or health professionals (non-M.D.).

It is to be hoped that those responsible for defining the goals of higher education and for selecting the best means of achieving those goals will do so with a full awareness of the alternatives available to them. This summary of findings on the impact of invisible colleges is intended to offer the kind of practical and empirically based information that is needed to make informed choices among educational alternatives.

7. Analysis and Recommendations

In this study, we have attempted to analyze the characteristics of the nearly 500 invisible colleges in this country, defining *invisibility* operationally as having a small and unselect student enrollment and being of private status. More specifically, we have examined the history of the invisible colleges [a large proportion of which began as (and some of which have remained) church-related]; their administrative characteristics; the characteristics of their students; their college environments or atmospheres; and the impact that they have on their students. Throughout, we have compared the invisible colleges with the elite private colleges (a group that is in many ways their polar opposite) and with the four-year public colleges (a group that constitutes their chief competition in the struggle to attract students, faculty, and funds). As we have seen, invisible colleges exist in all but three of the fifty states, and they enroll approximately 15 percent of all students attending four-year colleges. In addition, compared with other private colleges, they receive substantially less money from virtually all sources, including tuition, foundation grants, private gifts, and federal and state aid. Thus, we have been dealing with a considerable segment of American higher education that can properly be designated as "have-not" institutions.

From time to time, it is suggested that most of these invisible colleges should be allowed to decline and eventually to die out. Usually, the arguments behind this suggestion are that the invisible colleges are of poor quality, that they no longer serve a real mission, that they do not attract enough students to warrant their continued existence, that they duplicate the resources and functions of other higher education institutions, and that they are too inefficient and too wasteful to justify any attempt to keep afloat.

During the next two decades, the colleges and universities in this

93

country will no doubt face a serious financial crisis: where is the money to come from? Even in the late 1960s, many institutions, including the elite ones, were talking of poverty and imminent disaster; some state legislatures had already started to cut funds for higher education, not only imposing serious strains on the public sector but also stifling any hopes within the private sector that the states would provide increased aid. Given this pervasive mood of impending doom—and the hard fact that all this concern may be something more than idle and unwarranted pessimism[1]—what can be said about the place of the invisible college?

In this final chapter, we shall attempt to deal with the following questions. First, what is the specific plight of the invisible colleges? Second, in what ways, if any, do they justify their existence? Third, what might be done to salvage and strengthen them?

THE PLIGHT OF THE INVISIBLE COLLEGE

A common concern expressed by educators today is the "plight of the small college." To most educators, however, "the small college" has come to mean the elite college: the small private college with a national reputation for academic excellence. Our evidence suggests that the problems of the elite colleges are qualitatively different from those facing the invisible colleges. Elite colleges are, to be sure, caught in certain financial binds that may affect their programs, and as they continue to raise their already high tuition fees in order to support these high-cost programs, they may find it increasingly more difficult to maintain their high admissions standards. At the same time, they may find that their already affluent student clientele will comprise fewer and fewer students from poor families and from minority groups.

But these problems pale in comparison with those of the invisible colleges. For them, the question is not one of changes in the characteristics of their student bodies; it is a question of survival. They are not concerned about whether they will attract too many or too few students of a particular type but about whether they will attract enough students of any type. As Chapter 4 indicated, the students who attend invisible colleges are very similar (particularly in their rather low socioeconomic backgrounds) to the students who attend public colleges. Thus, it is safe to conclude that the proliferation of tax-subsidized public institutions poses a much greater threat

[1] See, for example, the recent report on the financial status of private colleges by Jellema (1971).

to the invisible college than to the elite one. The prospect of a virtually free public higher education is likely to be far more tempting to the prospective invisible college student than to the prospective elite college student.

At the heart of this dilemma is the confusion of the invisible college over its role and identity. So far, no one has developed a strategy for the salvation of invisible colleges that does not jeopardize either their small size or their private status. Therefore, salvation has rested in faith: faith in traditional purposes, faith in their Christian mission (in the case of church-related colleges), faith in the values of smallness and of freedom from state interference and control. But gradually, the invisible colleges have been drifting toward the model of the elite college, attempting to "upgrade" themselves by recruiting a more select student body from a wider geographical range, by attracting a more highly trained, research-oriented faculty, by disaffiliating themselves from their founding churches. These attempts to emulate the model of the elite college are perhaps more to be pitied than deplored, for they are almost certainly doomed to failure.

At present, the invisible colleges are plagued by inadequate federal and state aid and by their very small endowments. One administrator at an invisible college pinpointed this second problem as follows:

Our alumni do not support us well, since they are not generally in the upper earning class. Our graduates are service-oriented. They are well known in teaching, Boy Scouts, Goodwill Industries, and theological circles but, of course, are not rich. Therefore we need a source of *large* donations for operating expenses. So far we have been unable to find such donors, since our program is good but not considered unique in foundation circles.

As a consequence of this lack of outside financial support, the invisible colleges have become increasingly dependent upon tuition and fees for income. As the data in Chapter 3 indicate, the dollar tuition discrepancies between invisible and public colleges are much greater than those between invisible and elite colleges. Thus, the public colleges have the advantage of being able to attract more lower-income students who might otherwise attend invisible colleges, and the elite colleges have the advantage of their superior prestige to make higher tuition charges acceptable to their prospective students.

Another administrator at an invisible college in a small Midwestern state made the following observation:

We have been a private college, largely for students of our state, and in the past have competed fairly well on a cost basis with other area institutions. Rising costs and concurrent efforts to develop an outstanding faculty have priced our college out of its previous market. The percentage of students from our state is declining. It seems likely that the college will survive as a good, small liberal arts college, but to do so it must (and is beginning to) develop a student constituency on a much broader geographic base.

Short of raising tuitions and thus pricing themselves out of the market, the alternatives open to the invisible colleges in their efforts to remain solvent are generally unattractive. They can offer lower faculty salaries; they can use unrestricted endowment to meet operating costs; they can increase the ratio of students to faculty; or they can try to attract more students. (In the case of the institution just mentioned, it was decided to invest more money in faculty salaries. In the process, tuitions were raised, efforts were instituted to appeal to a more widespread group of prospective students, and faculty-student ratio was sacrificed.)

The major difficulties with most of these self-help strategies are (a) that they are not likely to work and (b) that even if they do, they are likely to be self-defeating in that they may very well erode the special contributions and essential virtues of the invisible colleges. It is to these topics—and to the basic question of whether the invisible colleges are worth saving—that we now turn.

HOW DO THE INVISIBLE COLLEGES JUSTIFY THEIR EXISTENCE? Most observers would agree that a status hierarchy exists in higher education whereby the elite colleges set the pace, the standards, and the goals for all four-year liberal arts colleges. The less prestigious colleges attempt to emulate the elite model not out of any educational design but out of a probably mistaken notion of what constitutes quality, thus abnegating their responsibility to carry out their own special missions. Since the invisible colleges are conspicuously lacking in most of the "elite" characteristics, it has become fashionable in some academic circles to express doubt that they are really "worth saving."

Putting aside, for a moment, the objection that these sweeping educational judgments are usually based not on any empirical evidence about the effects of various types of colleges but on ignorance that simply perpetuates the myths and prejudices of elitism, one may still seriously question whether it is in any way desirable to have all higher educational institutions aim for one or two "ideal" models. Whatever the virtues and defects of particular types of institutions, surely such a goal deserves to be challenged.

American higher education has long prided itself on its diversity. One of its fundamental assumptions has been that there are important individual differences among students in their talents, aspirations, interests, and educational needs. If one accepts this assumption, then it follows that some students will develop better in small colleges than in large ones, in church-related colleges than in nonsectarian ones, in unselective than in selective ones. In these circumstances, the ideal system is one that provides a variety of meaningful options designed to accommodate these individual differences.

Yet in some respects, this much-touted diversity is on the wane. Many of our larger colleges and universities, both public and private, are coming to resemble one another more and more: they are complex, impersonal, and alike in their curricular offerings. Moreover, these same colleges and universities are coming to serve an increasing proportion of the nation's students. Even institutions that were first established to provide specialized training—technological and vocational institutions, teachers colleges, agricultural colleges—have been bemused into believing that the aim of all higher educational institutions should be to turn out students who are "well-rounded," "humanized," and "cultured," and thus have added more and more required liberal arts courses to their curricula and allowed themselves to be diverted from their original purposes.

Under the relatively free market that existed in the early years of collegiate development, institutions whose educational programs did not appeal to sufficient numbers of students simply foundered. Institutions that survived were able to do so because they were meeting a demand for a certain kind of educational option. In recent years, however, with the development of the public sector, the free market no longer exists. In the face of what many invisible college administrators have alleged to be the educational equivalent of unfair price competition by public institutions, only the most prestigious private colleges and universities continue to attract more students than they can accommodate.

Unfortunately, it is virtually impossible to determine whether the invisible colleges that have closed down were forced to do so because they no longer provided meaningful educational options or because the cost squeeze was simply too much for them. It is not unreasonable to suppose, however, that if a free market were restored, many public institutions would have to make drastic changes in their programs to attract sufficient numbers of students. But with spiraling tuition fees at *all* types of private colleges, many of the students who might otherwise choose to go to invisible colleges are unable to take advantage of this option. Thus we have reached what many might deem, in the light of our past assumptions, an unhealthy situation, both from the standpoint of higher education in general and from the standpoint of the individual student. Our system is becoming more and more homogenized, and, concomitant with that, the options open to the student (and particularly the student of average or below average academic ability) are being closed off.

Of course, few people would push the concept of the virtues of diversity and heterogeneity to the reductio ad absurdum of maintaining that institutions that are demonstrably inferior and inefficient should be kept around just for the sake of providing options. Institutions that are plainly incompetent or that have what most people would agree are adverse effects on student development (though here, of course, one enters into the realm of value judgments about the objectives of higher education) have no particular "right" to survive or to ask for support. Let such institutions die their merciful deaths. But are the invisible colleges as a group demonstrably of "poor quality," "inefficient," and "redundant," as their detractors claim, merely because they do not live up to elitist standards? Surely, the evidence presented in Chapters 5 and 6 suggests that they have many favorable effects that neither the elite colleges nor the public four-year colleges can claim. To summarize briefly: The selectivity of the elite colleges seems to give the student no special educational advantages; his cognitive development would proceed just as well at a relatively unselective college. Moreover, these two types of colleges do not differ with respect to their impact on the student's educational progress or degree aspirations, though they do have some effect on career plans: elite colleges tend to divert their students toward the humanities and the social sciences, whereas invisible colleges seem to foster an interest in the physical sciences and the health professions.

Obviously, in this area, they are performing different functions, neither of which can be considered undesirable.

Looking at public four-year colleges, we find that though their students are more likely to express overall satisfaction with the college and are more likely to return to the college for the sophomore year, those who do drop out are less apt than the invisible college dropouts to reenroll immediately in some other institution. Moreover, many public four-year colleges suffer the infirmities of large institutions in general. Their students perceive them as cold and impersonal, contacts between faculty and students are rare, and the students themselves seem isolated from one another.

Perhaps the most important attribute shared by invisible and elite colleges is smallness. As the data in Chapter 5 indicate, the typical small college is characterized by a more friendly atmosphere, closer contacts between faculty and students, a stronger identification with the institution, and a feeling on the part of the students that they matter as individuals. Although it remains to be proven empirically that these institutional attributes are indeed virtues, one can make a strong a priori case that they are more conducive to student development than are the depersonalizing and alienating attributes of large institutions.

More simply, one can argue that smallness tends to preserve the student's sense of identity and to offer him a much wider range of meaningful opportunities. For example, the student at a small institution probably has a much better chance of taking part in certain types of extracurricular activities — student government, the campus newspaper, varsity athletics, and similar organizations — than does the student at a large institution, who may have many more such organizations to choose from but is likely to be competing with many more students for a position in any given one.

It is not our intention to imply that large institutions do not have their own virtues: larger libraries, more diverse curricula, better laboratory facilities, a wider offering of cultural events on campus. To some students, these opportunities may well prove more attractive than what invisible colleges have to offer. Nonetheless, in such matters as personal contacts with faculty members and with other students, the feeling of belonging, and the opportunity for participation in certain types of extracurricular activities, the student pays a certain price for the advantages of large size. Again, it comes down to a matter of individual differences and a range of options.

Preserving and strengthening the many diverse options represented by all types of colleges is essential to the well-being of our higher educational system.

Perhaps the most important *educational* justification for saving the invisible colleges is that they have the special expertise required to provide appropriate learning opportunities to many of the students who now make up a large segment of the expanding college population. From the point of view of public policy, the invisible college can be regarded as an underutilized educational resource. At a time when public institutions of all types are having major problems meeting the student demand for places, it is ironic that dozens of private colleges are in danger of extinction because of a dearth of student applicants. The irony becomes even greater when one realizes that the enrollment pressures on public colleges stem in part from an influx of students who are educationally disadvantaged and underprepared. Indeed, as was pointed out in Chapter 4, they resemble in many ways the typical students at the invisible colleges. Both groups tend to make mediocre grades in high school, to score low on aptitude tests, to come from poor socioeconomic backgrounds, and to have a strong interest in vocational as opposed to strictly academic curricula. There are, of course, some important differences. Invisible colleges are more likely to attract students from rural rather than urban backgrounds; and, except in the case of the black colleges, they recruit relatively few nonwhite students. (It should be pointed out, however, that by objective economic criteria, most disadvantaged students are white—H.S. Astin, 1970.)

To accommodate these students, many states and municipalities are moving toward a policy of open admissions, whereby the graduate of any secondary school in the area concerned is automatically granted admission upon application. Perhaps the strongest opposition to open admissions comes from those public institutions that have traditionally employed relatively stringent admissions criteria. The faculty frequently complain, with some justification, that their educational programs are geared to relatively advanced students and that serious disruption will result if masses of poorly prepared students are suddenly admitted. In addition, they argue, the experience will be detrimental to the disadvantaged students themselves, who might grow discouraged at their inability to keep up with the programs and lose their taste for higher education altogether. In all fairness, it should be pointed out that internal opposition to open admissions varies from state to state and even from institution to institution within a system. As Dunham (1969) points out, some educators at state institutions regard the brightness of a student as irrelevant; the mission of the college, as they see it, is to serve the needs of mass education. Others, particularly the younger Ph.D.'s on the faculty, regard the student's academic ability as decidedly relevant in that it contributes to the institution's status and thus in turn enhances their own reputations.

But whatever the attitudes of faculty and administrators toward open admissions, one can seriously question whether some state institutions have any special competence to deal with these students. Although 13 of the 50 states have traditionally had open admissions policies, many of the public institutions in other states that are now contemplating open admissions have traditionally employed selective admissions. And it is here that the invisible colleges can make a valuable contribution, because, in contrast to these more selective public colleges, they have already developed a staff and a program that is geared specifically to the needs of less academically able students. Consequently, they may be ideally suited to providing the opportunities needed by the wave of open-admissions students. Certainly it would seem an easier solution for the invisible colleges to broaden and perhaps modify their present programs than for the more selective public institutions to water down their present programs or to introduce whole new programs of special courses. In these circumstances, we believe that federal and state governments should give serious consideration to mechanisms for subsidizing either the students of invisible colleges or the institutions themselves, thereby taking some of the enrollment pressure off public institutions, infusing new life into moribund invisible colleges, and, most important of all, providing the student with the kind of educational options and experiences that will best satisfy his own abilities and needs.

RECOMMEN-DATIONS In light of the above discussion, it seems clear to us that, by and large, the invisible colleges justify their existence. In the first place, they help to maintain the diversity of our higher education system, in which each type of institution plays a distinctive role in the division of labor. Of course, all colleges and universities share in varying degrees the collective functions of teaching, research, and public service; but each institution must have its own priorities if the social and economic problems of our time are to be coped with effectively.

Invisible colleges, in addition to providing options not otherwise available, have special assets and virtues that contribute to higher education as a whole. They are small, and thus provide a warmer and more cohesive atmosphere than do large institutions; they give the student greater opportunities to participate in a number of activities; and, most significant, they have traditionally designed their programs to suit a student clientele that is in many respects similar to the less able and less well-prepared students who are currently imposing a heavy burden on the public institutions.

Those of the academic community who tend to denigrate all institutions that do not share the attributes of the elite institutions may very well resist the notion of attempting to "save" the invisible colleges. But, as has been pointed out frequently before, the traditional notions of what constitutes institutional excellence and effectiveness need to be carefully scrutinized and probably revised. We must consider the question from the perspective of the educational purposes of our colleges and universities, of the needs of our society, and of the individual differences in our college-age youth.

But granting that at least a fair portion of the 494 invisible institutions in the United States can and do perform a valuable function, we cannot escape the question of how to keep them solvent and at the same time preserve their distinctive characteristics. The most obvious answer is through outside aid, probably by the state. The question of state aid to private higher education is, of course, a thorny one, involving as it so often does the constitutional guarantees of religious freedom and the separation of church and state. Nonetheless, now that virtually all 50 states have established some sort of statewide coordinating board—ranging all the way from voluntary associations among institutions (definitely in the minority) to statewide governing boards with substantial powers —a new look is being taken at the possibility of bringing private higher education into the picture. As Berdahl puts it, "the push of several federal programs that require public-private cooperation and the pull of increasing economic distress in some private institutions have combined to make state relations with private higher education an issue of emerging importance" (1971, p. 201). Indeed, many statewide coordinating agencies include representatives of private institutions among their members, and it is coming to be recognized more and more that utilization of the resources of private institutions is, in the long run, a matter of best serving the public interest. Consequently, many states have attempted to find feasible means of providing various kinds of support to private institutions. In Iowa, for example, a formula is used to make up the difference between public and private institutions for in-state students. In effect, this method lays to rest the ghost of "unfair price competition." Other states provide scholarships that give the recipient free choice as to what type of institution he will attend. In still other states, support is given to institutions (public *and* private) that offer programs (for instance, in nursing) where the demand for manpower is high and where the supply of trained persons is low.

We recommend that each state — probably through its coordinating agency — make a thorough inventory of its own needs and of its educational resources that may help to fill those needs. Too often, the invisible colleges are overlooked in such a general assessment; it is high time that they were taken into consideration, since they have in the past and can in the future make significant contributions to the general welfare of the state.

Undoubtedly, the public sector, particularly the four-year colleges, will resist having "their" funds diverted to private institutions. But it should be possible for coordinating agencies — which ideally are in a position to balance the interests of the public institutions with the public interest — to provide long-term support to private institutions and, perhaps, to save the taxpayers of the state a substantial amount of money.

If the invisible colleges are to receive public support, one issue that must be faced squarely is that their very small enrollments may make for waste and inefficiency. As Table 5 (Chapter 1) indicates, more than 70 percent of the invisible colleges have fewer than 1,000 students; 50 percent have fewer than 750. These figures suggest that many invisible colleges may be superfluous and too expensive to be kept in business.

Is it possible that invisible colleges could substantially increase their enrollments without jeopardizing the advantages of their small size? Although the research evidence here is not entirely clear, it would seem that when one gets below the 2,500 enrollment figure, differences in size do not have any major effects on the institutional environment. Thus, it would seem desirable for invisible colleges enrolling fewer than 1,000 students to consider expanding their enrollments by several hundred students.

The arguments in favor of such expansion are primarily economic. It is just too costly to maintain administrative staff, libraries, buildings, laboratories, residence halls, and so forth, when the student body is very small. Moreover, if an institution enrolling 600 students increases its income 50 percent simply by enrolling another 300 students, it does not, at the same time, increase its expenditures by 50 percent, particularly if its existing facilities (dormitories, classrooms, etc.) are already underutilized, as is the case at many invisible colleges. In short, there would seem to be every reason to encourage the very small colleges to increase their enrollments by 50 percent or even more; financial incentives might well be the best means of encouragement.

In several states contracts have been developed between the public sector and individual private institutions whereby funds are provided to the private institutions to expand their enrollments, thus relieving some of the pressures on public institutions. Such contractual arrangements should, of course, be made known to prospective students beforehand, so that they can decide, at the time they apply to the public institution, whether they will accept assignment to one of the contracting private institutions.

From the practical point of view, it is essential to show that state-subsidized expansion of private colleges is a more efficient and economical way of coping with increasing enrollments than the expansion of existing public institutions or the creation of new ones. Our data in Table 21 (Chapter 3) indicate that the per-student costs of operating invisible colleges are somewhat greater than those involved in operating public two-year and four-year colleges. But these figures may be somewhat misleading, since they do not reflect the substantial capital expenditures required to expand existing institutions or build new ones. It should also be pointed out that the higher operating costs of the typical invisible college are partly attributable to the expense of maintaining residence halls and related facilities; at public institutions (particularly community colleges), these expenses are usually not so high, since more students live at home and commute to campus. Moreover, such costs would not, presumably, be included in public subsidies to the invisible colleges.

The real picture here is, to be sure, a bit murky. It would be useful if those states that are now considering the possibility of increasing subsidies to private colleges would calculate the expense involved relative to the expense of expanding the public sector. When capital costs are included, and when the costs of operating residential facilities are considered separately, it may well turn out in many states that giving subsidies to private institutions is the less expensive of the two alternatives. The data in Chapter 5 indicate that the economies might be greatest with respect to subsidies to the invisible colleges, whose operating costs are substantially lower than those of other types of private colleges.

It is interesting to speculate on the potential capacity of the invisible colleges to absorb some of the expanding enrollment pressures now being felt in the public sector. The population of new college freshmen (first-time, full-time students) increases each year by approximately 65,000 students. If each of the 494 invisible colleges could be persuaded to take in an average of, say, 100 of these new students in a given year, and if another 150 of the least visible "middle" colleges could each be persuaded to take on the same number, it would be unnecessary for the public institutions to expand their facilities *at all* that year.

On a more modest level, the pressures could still be reduced by half if each invisible college were to take in only 50 additional new students. If this number were to be increased to 100 by the next year and to 150 by the third year, the invisible colleges could continue to absorb half of the enrollment increase over the next three years. If the figure of 150 were maintained in subsequent years, the maximum increase in the size of the total student enrollment — even allowing for only minimal attrition — would almost certainly not exceed 500 students at any invisible college. Moreover, the enrollment, even with this increase, would still be well below 2,000 students in most cases, so the advantages of small size would probably not be sacrificed.

A much more ambitious alternative is to subsidize each invisible college so that it can embark upon a carefully planned program of expansion, reaching a target enrollment of, say, 1,800 students within a period of three to five years. In this way, the invisible colleges alone (leaving out the middle colleges altogether) could accommodate close to 400,000 additional undergraduates, which is about 80 percent of the total projected increase in undergraduate enrollment during the next four years.

If additional funds are to be invested in the invisible colleges, we believe that they should be used to improve the teaching-learning process rather than simply to ape the elitist model by adding more Ph.D.'s to the faculty, raising admissions standards, expanding the library, and so forth. In the first place, American higher education is already well supplied with elite models; indeed, there is probably already too little diversity in programs and standards of excellence. In the second place, even with massive infusions of new money, any attempt on the part of invisible colleges to achieve the affluence and prestige necessary to move into the elite class is bound to fail. The gaps between them—in student ability levels, faculty training, and financial resources—are too great to be bridged. Therefore, efforts to "upgrade" invisible colleges along traditional elitist lines should be discouraged.

In seeking public support for invisible colleges, it might be possible to convince legislators that subsidies should be based on an institution's lack of selectivity; preference might be given to those institutions whose entering students' high school grades and ability test scores fall below a certain level. In this way, state funds would go to private institutions that are in the greatest need, giving them a positive incentive to broaden and strengthen educational programs geared to students in the lower ability ranges and deterring them from raising admissions standards.

We recognize that, in spite of these arguments, invisible colleges will be subjected to intensive internal pressures to strive for elitist status. Moreover, these pressures will be augmented by certain outside forces—for example, regional accrediting associations— which may have difficulty adjusting to any criteria of institutional excellence or effectiveness other than the conventional ones.

For these reasons, we would qualify our recommendation by saying that public aid should probably not take the form of unrestricted general support. Rather, we would recommend that public funds be granted only with the provision that they be used to preserve and strengthen an institution's unique educational programs, to make modest increases in enrollment, and to develop innovative programs designed for less able or poorly prepared students.

Employing this same approach, most of the funds allocated under Title III of the Higher Education Act of 1965 were devoted to curriculum development, particularly for students in the lower ability levels. One of the most successful Title III programs was the Thirteen Colleges Curriculum Development Project administered by the Institute for Services to Education. Addressed primarily to the freshman and sophomore levels, this project indicated that attrition could be reduced and academic motivation increased among the students taking part in the program. A similar program is required for the invisible colleges, inasmuch as they have the appropriate environment for encouraging students who need extra help and for focusing primarily on teaching rather than research.

Our remarks should not be taken to mean that we feel invisible colleges should not be improved in other ways. Institutions of all types must constantly work to improve their particular programs and to fulfill their special missions more completely. What we do want to emphasize is that the focus should be on improving the teaching and learning process, especially for disadvantaged students.

What is needed, then, is a thorough examination — both by those concerned with public policy at the state and federal level and by those in the academic world — of the invisible college's mission and role in higher education and of its particular strengths. More than that, we need to take a closer look at our entire system of higher education, at the advantages of its diversity, and at the contributions that various types of colleges can make. Perhaps such scrutiny will ultimately lead to a wider view of what constitutes institutional excellence, a view based on educational values rather than on tradition, sentiment, and academic snobbery.

Commentary

East of the Mississippi, where American higher education began, very little attention has been given to the overall structure of higher education until quite recently. Historically, the basic structure grew out of a variety of independent forces and beliefs; institutional evolution was largely unrelated to and uncoordinated with other higher education. Then came the midcentury postwar era with three powerful forces which have altered both the status of our collegiate institutions and their overall structure: one has been the pressure for the expansion of higher education, a result of the increasing number of skills needed to manage accelerating complexity and technology; another has been the sheer impact of numbers resulting from a compound of a higher percentage of college aspirants and a greater number of people of college age; a third, the result of the first two, has been the accumulation of groups of students whose background, competence, academic interest, and skill requirements cover an ever-expanding range of variables.

The dominant reaction to these forces has been a very widespread adoption of some form of the California system of comprehensive community colleges, four-year state colleges, and major state universities. Both the structure and the operation of these new behemoths have moved in the direction of standardization and away from the need for even greater pluralism in the present.

The increasing standardization of higher education is a direct result of state governmental control. The explosive demand for college stations since World War II could not be satisfied by the independent institutions. When the student growth problem was largely taken over by the states, the programs everywhere included the same tax subsidy that had always characterized state institutions. This, of course, made it more economical for students to attend the tax-supported community college, state college, or state university than to attend the independent institution. The rapid inflation of college costs, to say nothing of family costs, has accelerated the growth trend of the tax-supported institution relative to that of the independent institution.

Within this matrix the invisible colleges are struggling for existence in a culture that stoutly proclaims a belief in educational pluralism and increasingly fails to support it.

The need for pluralism in higher education is importantly affected by a great many things. Chief among the variables is the infinite range of goals and objectives set forth by the students themselves (and their parents). These are compounded by ethnic background, home influence, primary and secondary school quality, health, motivation, finances, race, and, perhaps, many other factors.

In addition to this array of factors, the need for higher training has expanded the intellectual band which traditionally has been the prime criterion in selective admissions. Fewer than 9 percent of our total population have IQ's of 120 and above. Only 16 percent are in the band between 110 and 119, and 50 percent of the population fall between 90 and 110.[1] If one-half of our people, or more, are going to college, it is quite obvious that the bulk of them will not be the elite intellects with IQ scores of 120 or above. It would seem equally obvious that if we are going to educate a great bulk of people whose IQ's range from 90 to 120, we ought to give them both quality education and the particular type of education they desire.

When the expanding intellectual range factor is added to the other variables, the importance of a careful factual analysis of the invisible colleges and their contribution becomes apparent. A goodly number of these institutions were founded or have evolved to their present status for the very reason that there has always been a pluralistic institutional need to meet pluralistic individual demands.

Whether the invisible colleges have fulfilled their mission well is a troublesome question. The disturbing array of facts in this book indicates the known quality defects of the invisible colleges as measured by traditional standards. Of even greater interest is the disturbing question of what constitutes quality in higher education.

---

[1] See David Wechsler: *Measurement and Appraisal of Adult Intelligence,* Williams and Wilkins, Baltimore, 4th ed., 1958.

The startling revelation that the good students do about as well in the poor schools as they do in the good schools shatters some ancient myths and certainly indicates the need for some refined semantics. Is quality education only high-quality training of high-quality minds? Or is it also quality training of average minds? Which school has higher-quality education, one that does a superb job on an average mind or one that does an average job on a superb mind? When one reads the intriguing statistical development and commentary in the foregoing pages these questions clearly come to mind.

The report is based largely on data pertaining to a very short span of time. Similar data covering a longer period of time would be very enlightening as an indication of trends and a delineation of the long-range services the invisible colleges have performed. One such service in this category has been the training of the majority of today's Negro teachers and community leaders, a service accomplished in spite of the problems and troubles of the predominantly black colleges. It would seem quite socially wasteful to permit the experience and going-concern value of these and the other invisible institutions to disappear. But disappear they may.

There has been a surprising mortality of colleges in the past. It could happen again. As the text points out, there are those who advocate a survival-of-the-fittest philosophy in determining the desirability of continued existence. This approach fails in two respects. First, it overlooks the fact that society as a whole pays the total costs of all higher education whether the form be gifts, tuition, or taxes. It is misleading, therefore, to impute merit to a showing of competitive strength that is largely based on a social subsidy. The destruction of many of the invisible colleges through indifference to the impact of their subsidized competition may actually be costly on a dollar basis alone. Aside from this, a total educational plan for a society should be based on an analysis of real needs. If some of the colleges which cannot survive under the somewhat ruthless survival-of-the-fittest conditions are actually rendering service that the surviving colleges do not render, a well-organized society should be ingenious enough either to preserve these institutions and the services they render or to provide the services in a better way by a new structure. The authors of *The Invisible Colleges* have carefully pointed out a set of real values unique to the invisible colleges or at least to many of them, values which justify major efforts for their preservation.

The traditional thinking about higher education has always been laced with myth and emotion. Someone has pointed out that most people's views of colleges are autobiographical. It is refreshing to find an analysis keyed to a carefully researched foundation of facts; it is doubly refreshing to have it so clearly expressed.

Ralph M. Besse

References

Astin, Alexander W.: *The College Environment,* American Council on Education, Washington, D.C., 1968a.

Astin, Alexander W.: "College Impact on Student Attitudes and Behavior," paper presented at the annual meeting of the American Educational Research Association, New York, February 6, 1971a.

Astin, Alexander W.: "An Empirical Characterization of Higher Educational Institutions," *Journal of Educational Psychology,* vol. 53, pp. 224–235, October 1962.

Astin, Alexander W.: "Further Validation of the Environmental Assessment Technique," *Journal of Educational Psychology,* vol. 54, pp. 217–226, August 1963.

Astin, Alexander W.: "Institutional Selectivity and Institutional Outcomes," paper presented at the 137th meeting of the American Association for the Advancement of Science, Chicago, December 27, 1970a.

Astin, Alexander W.: *Manual for the Inventory of College Activities,* National Computer Systems, Inc., Minneapolis, 1971b.

Astin, Alexander W.: "The Methodology of Research on College Impact, Part One," *Sociology of Education,* vol. 43, pp. 223–254, Summer 1970b.

Astin, Alexander W.: "Patterns of 'Quality' in Graduate Education," American Council on Education, Washington, D.C., 1970c. (Unpublished manuscript.)

Astin, Alexander W.: *Predicting Academic Performance in College,* The Free Press, New York, 1971c.

Astin, Alexander W.: "Racial Considerations in Admissions," in David C. Nichols and Olive Mills (eds.), *The Campus and the Racial Crisis,* American Council on Education, Washington, D.C., 1970d, pp. 113–141.

Astin, Alexander W.: "Undergraduate Achievement and Institutional 'Excellence,'" *Science,* vol. 161, pp. 661–668, August 16, 1968b.

Astin, Alexander W.: *Who Goes Where to College?*, Science Research Associates, Inc., Chicago, 1965.

Astin, Alexander W., and Alan E. Bayer: "Antecedents and Consequents of Disruptive Campus Protests," *Measurement and Evaluation in Guidance,* vol. 4, no. 1, pp. 18–30, April 1971.

Astin, Alexander W., and John L. Holland: "The Distribution of 'Wealth' in Higher Education," *College and University,* vol. 37, pp. 113–125, Winter 1962.

Astin, Alexander W., and John L. Holland: "The Environmental Assessment Technique (EAT): A Way to Measure College Environments," *Journal of Educational Psychology,* vol. 52, pp. 308–316, December 1961.

Astin, Alexander W., and Robert J. Panos: *The Educational and Vocational Development of College Students,* American Council on Education, Washington, D.C., 1969.

Astin, Alexander W., Robert J. Panos, and John A. Creager: "A Program of Longitudinal Research on the Higher Educational System," *ACE Research Reports,* vol. 1, no. 1, American Council on Education, Washington, D.C., 1966.

Astin, Helen S.: *Educational Progress of Disadvantaged Students,* University Research Corporation, Human Service Press, Washington, D.C., 1970.

Bayer, Alan E., and Alexander W. Astin: "Violence and Disruption on the U.S. Campus, 1968–69," *Educational Record,* vol. 50, pp. 337–350, Fall 1969.

Bayer, Alan E., and Robert F. Boruch: "The Black Student in American Colleges," *ACE Research Reports,* vol. 4, no. 2, American Council on Education, Washington, D.C., 1969.

Berdahl, Robert O.: *Statewide Coordination of Higher Education,* American Council on Education, Washington, D.C., 1971.

Brubacher, John S., and Willis Rudy: *Higher Education in Transition: An American History, 1636–1956,* Harper and Brothers, New York, 1958.

Cartter, Allan M.: *An Assessment of Quality in Graduate Education,* American Council on Education, Washington, D.C., 1966.

Cass, James, and Max Birnbaum: *Comparative Guide to American Colleges, 1970–71 Edition,* Harper & Row, Publishers, Incorporated, New York, 1969.

College Entrance Examination Board: *Manual of Freshman Class Profiles, 1967–69,* New York, 1967.

Creager, John A., Alexander W. Astin, Robert F. Boruch, Alan E. Bayer, and David E. Drew: "National Norms for Entering College Freshmen— Fall 1969," *ACE Research Reports,* vol. 4, no. 7, American Council on Education, Washington, D.C., 1969.

Dunham, E. Alden: *Colleges of the Forgotten Americans: A Profile of State Colleges and Regional Universities,* McGraw-Hill Book Company, New York, 1969.

Gleason, Phillip: "American Catholic Higher Education: A Historical Perspective," in Robert Hassenger (ed.), *The Shape of Catholic Higher Education,* University of Chicago Press, Chicago, 1967.

Gleazer, Edmund J., Jr. (ed.): *American Junior Colleges,* 7th edition, American Council on Education, Washington, D.C., 1967.

Gross, John O.: *Methodist Beginnings in Higher Education,* The Methodist Church, Board of Education, Division of Educational Institutions, Nashville, 1959.

Hassenger, Robert (ed.): *The Shape of Catholic Higher Education,* University of Chicago Press, Chicago, 1967.

Jellema, William: *The Red and the Black: Special Preliminary Report on the Financial Status, Present and Projected, of Private Institutions of Higher Learning,* Association of American Colleges, Washington, D.C., 1971.

Jencks, Christopher, and David Riesman: *The American Revolution,* Doubleday and Company, Inc., New York, 1968.

McGrath, Earl J.: *The Predominantly Negro Colleges and Universities in Transition,* Columbia University, Teachers College, New York, 1965.

Nichols, Robert C.: "Effects of Various College Characteristics on Student Aptitude Test Scores," *Journal of Educational Psychology,* vol. 55, pp. 45–54, February 1964.

Nichols, Robert C.: "Personality Change and the College," *American Educational Research Journal,* vol. 4, pp. 173–90, May 1967.

O'Connor, Brian, Jr.: "A Descriptive Survey of Colleges in the United States Belonging to the Association of Episcopal Colleges," doctoral dissertation, Association of Episcopal Colleges, New York, 1969.

Pace, C. Robert: *College and University Environmental Scales,* Educational Testing Service, Princeton, N.J., 1963.

Pace, C. Robert, and George G. Stern: "An Approach to the Measurement of Psychological Characteristics of College Environments," *Journal of Educational Psychology,* vol. 49, pp. 269–277, October 1958.

Patillo, Manning M., Jr., and Donald M. MacKenzie: *Church-Sponsored*

Higher Education in the United States: Report of the Danforth Commission, American Council on Education, Washington, D.C., 1966.

Peterson, Richard E.: "The Scope of Organized Student Protest in 1967–68," Educational Testing Service, Princeton, N.J., 1968. (Unpublished manuscript.)

Rock, Donald A., John A. Centra, and Robert L. Linn: "Relationships Between College Characteristics and Student Achievement," *American Educational Research Journal,* vol. 7, pp. 109–121, January 1970.

Singletary, Otis A. (ed.): *American Universities and Colleges,* 10th edition, American Council on Education, Washington, D.C., 1968.

U.S. Office of Education: *Advance Report on Opening Fall Enrollment in Higher Education, 1970: Institutional Data,* by George H. Wade, Report OE-54050-70, National Center for Educational Statistics, Washington, D.C., 1970.

U.S. Office of Education: *Education Directory, 1967–1968, Part 3: Higher Education,* U.S. Government Printing Office, Washington, D.C., 1968*a.*

U.S. Office of Education: HEGIS-II Reference File, 1968*b.*

Wicke, Myron F.: *The Church-Related College,* Center for Applied Research in Education, Inc., Washington, D.C., 1964.

Wiggins, Sam P.: *Higher Education in the South,* McCutchan Publishing Corporation, Berkeley, 1966.

Appendix A: Raw Data

Tables A-1 to A-4 show data on the entering freshman classes at each of 40 invisible and 23 elite colleges. These data, which were obtained from the students at the time of registration or freshman orientation in the fall of 1969, were collected in connection with the Cooperative Institutional Research Program of the American Council on Education (see Astin, Panos, & Creager, 1966).

TABLE A-1 *Raw data for the entering freshman classes at 40 invisible colleges, 1969*

Institution	Public school	Top 10% of class	Planning Ph.D.	Planning M.D.	Planning LL.B.	Less than 51 miles from home	Grew up on farm	Father's education post-graduate
01	89.0	11.4	8.5	3.0	1.2	19.4	6.7	9.1
02	95.4	54.8	23.1	5.6	5.0	25.8	10.6	1.9
03	88.8	39.9	13.5	5.7	0.9	10.6	16.3	9.1
04	46.8	40.4	13.4	0.0	0.0	42.2	5.9	10.4
05	45.2	18.5	5.0	2.3	0.5	18.5	4.4	21.1
06	70.7	42.6	5.4	0.5	0.0	4.8	15.5	2.7
07	96.9	47.1	19.9	2.1	1.4	48.6	7.8	2.9
08	86.1	14.3	10.5	1.2	0.0	57.0	1.2	12.8
09	86.2	22.4	5.9	0.0	0.0	44.5	0.6	15.0
10	28.2	8.6	10.0	4.7	1.4	8.2	4.2	8.1
11	96.9	18.4	8.7	4.3	0.7	33.4	30.4	7.3
12	93.1	13.2	10.6	2.7	0.5	22.0	17.5	12.7
13	87.5	11.7	11.7	0.7	0.7	39.6	6.5	8.1
14	94.4	20.9	9.1	3.2	1.3	19.3	13.7	8.5
15	50.0	29.2	5.7	0.7	0.0	21.8	25.0	5.7
16	98.6	27.1	11.4	5.4	0.0	26.3	29.5	11.0
17	93.9	52.5	16.6	4.5	1.0	14.0	38.2	3.2
18	19.0	23.9	9.6	3.1	1.4	79.6	3.8	3.1
19	24.7	27.4	11.2	2.2	1.1	23.2	1.1	19.8
20	95.9	27.7	6.5	2.9	1.0	17.2	9.7	14.1
21	26.1	22.0	11.1	3.4	0.4	32.0	8.0	8.8
22	47.1	24.6	4.2	1.4	0.0	68.1	2.8	4.2
23	97.1	33.3	8.1	1.4	1.4	18.6	17.6	9.6
24	87.5	22.1	4.9	1.5	0.3	4.2	4.7	23.3
25	94.7	21.3	11.2	5.6	1.4	15.5	11.7	15.2
26	30.3	33.8	16.6	8.5	2.4	34.9	2.4	14.9
27	41.5	7.1	4.5	0.0	0.0	95.3	0.0	6.8
28	96.6	33.2	21.1	3.5	0.3	13.2	11.4	4.8
29	73.8	45.7	6.1	2.2	0.0	6.9	3.3	25.4
30	89.8	18.3	5.3	5.3	1.1	11.4	10.5	15.1
31	88.6	35.6	25.3	10.6	1.9	13.3	1.1	25.9
32	22.0	16.9	12.0	5.7	3.6	9.9	2.1	9.8
33	45.1	33.1	6.2	5.1	0.4	17.9	55.2	10.9

Race– white	Religious background Jewish	Religious background Roman Catholic	Parental income $6,000	Scholar-ship	Major concern re financing	Current politics left or liberal	Current politics moderate or strongly conservative
97.0	6.3	28.8	10.0	15.2	6.7	27.9	39.3
0.0	0.0	5.8	66.2	60.5	21.1	42.0	52.9
98.3	0.0	0.9	14.0	12.0	12.3	19.3	48.0
82.1	0.0	73.5	12.7	34.8	5.9	34.9	23.8
95.2	0.0	86.0	8.7	23.2	12.9	34.3	16.9
90.9	7.3	27.9	35.1	65.4	17.6	28.8	17.9
0.0	0.0	1.8	53.8	20.1	25.6	33.2	27.4
76.7	1.2	24.7	18.6	40.7	15.1	46.8	16.4
88.3	32.2	28.9	9.7	35.7	9.7	38.5	21.7
96.5	0.2	91.6	8.6	13.0	17.0	36.8	17.3
99.3	1.4	16.5	14.7	30.9	7.2	26.4	21.7
95.8	0.0	12.2	10.3	17.4	18.0	39.6	23.0
90.6	5.8	29.0	17.0	43.3	16.7	33.9	17.3
95.5	0.6	23.4	14.7	24.5	12.9	25.0	22.9
99.3	0.0	82.0	21.6	31.2	24.1	31.0	19.7
87.9	1.4	4.8	23.6	24.8	16.2	30.0	18.6
83.7	0.0	5.3	65.7	21.7	16.7	25.4	22.9
97.9	0.3	92.4	15.9	32.2	22.3	37.6	16.4
86.7	0.0	88.8	15.3	26.4	6.7	30.5	25.7
98.0	0.8	13.5	6.4	23.2	11.5	28.4	25.6
96.2	0.0	94.7	11.5	40.6	14.8	37.5	23.0
93.1	0.0	97.2	20.0	37.5	11.1	36.2	15.9
85.1	0.0	2.8	31.3	13.3	18.7	23.1	46.4
97.5	8.0	12.6	2.3	8.5	4.6	29.9	25.1
84.0	0.7	13.9	20.1	44.5	21.4	33.1	30.1
97.9	0.0	94.1	7.9	29.3	8.7	42.7	20.6
100.0	0.0	93.2	21.4	4.5	9.1	35.7	37.5
0.0	0.0	2.2	51.1	52.0	23.5	23.7	21.2
99.4	0.6	3.4	2.4	7.7	1.7	19.5	38.9
85.3	5.4	30.1	17.6	26.3	9.5	33.3	16.1
0.0	0.3	11.5	21.7	32.9	11.4	62.9	22.0
89.6	0.0	92.1	10.9	19.6	9.8	33.0	29.5
97.3	0.0	0.0	26.2	26.3	16.2	18.0	29.9

TABLE A-1 *(continued)*

Institution	Public school	Top 10% of class	Planning Ph.D.	Planning M.D.	Planning LL.B.	Less than 51 miles from home	Grew up on farm	Father's education post-graduate
34	96.5	24.8	19.2	4.0	0.4	25.4	7.9	2.6
35	90.0	10.5	14.8	4.3	1.0	5.5	5.2	14.3
36	43.8	31.9	8.0	0.0	2.0	50.1	8.0	8.0
37	84.3	10.9	5.0	2.9	1.4	14.2	6.4	12.1
38	90.9	9.4	5.5	2.4	0.0	13.5	4.8	11.3
39	78.9	20.5	2.4	3.7	0.0	7.9	35.4	8.5
40	24.1	14.1	9.4	3.1	1.6	87.9	0.0	7.7
Highest	98.6	54.8	25.3	10.6	5.0	95.3	55.2	25.9
Lowest	19.0	4.1	2.4	0.0	0.0	4.2	0.0	1.9
Mean	70.9	25.5	10.4	3.2	0.9	28.0	11.2	10.6
Mean-Catholic	34.4	22.9	9.2	2.7	1.1	44.0	5.2	9.9
Mean-Protestant	88.9	25.8	10.7	3.6	0.8	18.9	16.8	10.5
Mean-nonsectarian	87.6	28.4	11.4	3.2	1.0	22.8	9.4	11.9

Race– white	Religious background Jewish	Religious background Roman Catholic	Parental income $6,000	Scholar- ship	Major concern re financing	Current politics left or liberal	Current politics moderate or strongly conservative
0.4	0.4	2.6	46.3	30.2	17.0	38.1	19.5
94.3	0.5	17.8	10.5	23.6	9.4	31.1	21.6
96.0	0.0	90.0	6.6	26.0	20.0	34.7	28.6
97.9	2.9	26.6	12.0	22.1	13.7	27.4	26.0
92.4	5.5	38.8	16.5	30.0	15.3	34.4	21.4
93.9	0.0	0.0	16.7	9.8	13.4	20.0	36.0
100.0	0.0	90.8	6.4	40.0	13.8	41.4	37.9
100.0	32.2	94.7	66.2	65.4	25.6	62.9	52.9
0.0	0.0	0.0	2.3	4.5	1.7	18.0	15.9
81.5	2.0	38.3	20.0	28.0	14.0	33.1	26.0
94.6	0.0	88.3	12.9	27.6	13.5	35.9	24.1
83.5	0.9	10.1	21.4	23.4	14.4	28.4	29.1
70.5	6.6	21.5	27.0	36.5	13.8	37.6	23.4

TABLE A-2   *Raw data for the entering freshman classes at 23 elite colleges, 1969*

Institution	Public school	Top 10% of class	Planning Ph.D.	Planning M.D.	Planning LL.B.	Less than 51 miles from home	Grew up on farm	Father's education post-graduate
01	89.6	96.4	87.8	2.0	1.0	15.6	4.6	18.7
02	83.6	90.9	70.3	0.9	0.9	31.8	0.9	15.3
03	85.3	77.7	27.7	14.6	4.2	43.8	3.5	27.4
04	60.7	59.7	11.9	3.9	2.2	11.3	1.4	27.2
05	25.7	52.2	14.8	6.0	5.5	11.6	0.5	33.3
06	88.5	34.9	7.9	2.6	3.1	3.2	3.2	47.6
07	84.5	58.2	17.1	0.0	3.0	7.3	1.6	23.6
08	66.1	58.4	25.9	14.6	9.7	7.8	5.2	29.5
09	79.0	66.1	19.1	8.2	3.2	6.6	2.6	24.6
10	65.1	79.6	41.8	15.0	8.8	6.3	1.4	42.5
11	74.7	82.2	22.1	6.6	2.6	6.2	1.7	40.4
12	57.6	63.9	30.4	17.4	9.0	3.2	2.1	39.2
13	81.5	86.5	37.3	9.5	2.9	8.9	4.0	50.3
14	73.1	74.2	30.8	16.0	16.2	3.8	3.3	31.1
15	61.6	73.2	24.7	8.6	4.7	5.9	3.2	39.4
16	90.5	86.4	13.6	4.5	0.0	28.6	0.0	9.1
17	82.4	81.3	41.7	8.7	3.5	5.3	1.8	49.5
18	73.2	77.0	50.2	4.0	1.8	6.7	2.9	49.2
19	82.4	60.1	20.9	11.4	12.5	9.3	2.6	29.5
20	66.5	74.4	52.7	16.8	7.8	22.7	2.3	47.4
21	66.2	79.4	45.4	10.1	5.4	15.3	2.1	51.5
22	62.0	46.0	17.2	2.8	1.1	4.1	3.3	43.3
23	58.2	59.4	24.9	5.2	2.2	2.6	3.1	38.0
Highest	90.5	96.4	87.8	17.4	16.2	43.8	5.2	51.5
Lowest	25.7	34.9	7.9	0.9	0.0	2.6	0.0	9.1
Mean	72.0	70.3	32.0	8.6	4.8	11.6	2.3	35.1

Race–white	Religious background Jewish	Religious background Roman Catholic	Parental income $6,000	Scholar-ship	Major concern re financing	Current politics left or liberal	Current politics moderate or strongly conservative
91.3	12.3	16.9	7.2	65.2	5.1	48.9	13.9
83.8	4.6	11.0	7.2	52.3	10.8	39.9	32.4
88.7	4.5	14.5	6.7	19.7	8.3	46.5	24.7
96.8	12.0	23.5	4.9	22.9	8.6	50.9	15.4
96.8	0.0	96.3	3.3	27.0	5.8	47.1	22.7
92.5	13.2	11.7	5.2	30.5	10.4	74.8	9.9
97.5	4.2	27.5	6.7	27.1	9.9	44.7	20.3
87.3	6.8	34.5	6.0	33.6	6.3	43.2	25.7
95.5	9.0	24.8	5.8	18.1	9.3	50.4	20.1
91.6	18.4	16.1	4.2	25.4	3.4	59.8	17.5
94.4	10.1	20.7	3.0	19.4	8.5	49.3	22.3
90.6	10.0	22.7	7.3	27.0	3.0	49.2	23.0
91.8	5.7	13.4	4.5	36.6	3.4	55.8	16.9
89.7	9.4	23.1	8.4	37.7	4.5	46.9	27.2
93.1	17.2	24.8	7.2	27.7	9.7	65.3	14.8
100.0	9.5	29.6	0.0	59.1	0.0	38.1	42.9
92.1	26.9	8.7	3.7	29.7	5.9	75.2	5.3
92.9	15.8	9.1	7.7	27.3	11.3	88.6	4.6
93.1	11.9	9.7	3.5	24.9	5.7	48.5	18.9
87.2	23.8	19.2	7.5	35.5	1.7	78.8	5.8
86.2	16.7	14.2	5.7	34.8	4.0	68.1	7.4
95.7	23.4	8.7	3.6	16.5	9.1	86.9	3.8
95.2	4.1	19.5	4.1	17.9	5.7	53.6	14.9
100.0	26.9	96.3	8.4	65.2	11.3	88.6	42.9
83.8	0.0	8.7	0.0	16.5	0.0	38.1	3.8
88.4	11.7	21.7	5.4	31.1	6.5	57.0	17.8

TABLE A-3 *Career plans of entering freshman classes at 40 invisible colleges, 1969*

Institution	Artist	Business-man	Clergy-man	College teacher	Doctor	Educator (secondary)	Elem. teacher
01	5.7	27.2	1.9	2.5	3.8	21.5	6.3
02	6.8	6.2	0.0	4.1	2.7	19.2	8.9
03	6.1	8.1	6.1	3.5	6.6	19.1	7.8
04	12.1	4.5	1.5	4.5	0.0	10.6	24.2
05	14.3	0.9	0.5	0.0	1.8	10.6	18.0
06	4.6	6.4	1.2	2.9	2.3	20.2	8.7
07	7.1	19.2	0.8	3.4	1.5	16.2	11.7
08	2.3	2.3	4.7	3.5	0.0	25.6	1.2
09	1.4	0.0	0.0	0.7	0.0	12.3	76.7
10	2.6	23.4	4.8	0.5	3.8	17.5	7.9
11	5.9	15.4	0.0	0.0	2.9	26.5	10.3
12	7.2	14.4	4.4	1.1	1.1	22.1	14.4
13	11.3	13.5	0.0	1.5	0.8	17.3	9.8
14	2.8	13.1	2.1	2.8	3.4	21.4	6.9
15	8.8	4.4	0.0	0.0	0.7	22.8	8.8
16	2.2	6.5	1.4	0.7	2.9	19.6	9.4
17	5.1	7.2	0.8	2.1	3.3	22.1	5.4
18	5.7	24.1	2.1	0.7	3.9	16.7	7.1
19	9.2	8.0	0.0	0.0	2.3	11.5	10.3
20	5.0	10.8	0.5	1.3	2.6	23.9	23.2
21	7.8	8.5	5.0	1.9	4.3	15.5	14.3
22	6.0	0.0	3.0	0.0	0.0	16.4	19.4
23	8.7	1.4	7.2	2.9	0.0	15.9	17.4
24	28.5	5.1	0.0	0.4	0.8	5.7	9.2
25	7.4	9.6	1.5	4.4	5.9	21.3	9.6
26	3.9	13.3	0.5	1.7	8.5	15.0	2.7
27	0.0	2.4	2.4	0.0	0.0	12.2	75.6
28	6.4	13.4	0.7	2.7	2.3	10.4	7.4
29	9.6	0.6	0.0	3.4	2.8	10.1	11.2
30	16.3	13.0	0.0	0.0	5.4	29.3	7.6
31	9.8	6.4	0.0	1.2	10.4	10.1	6.9
32	4.3	27.1	1.6	1.1	4.8	9.6	8.0
33	4.3	7.0	2.0	0.8	4.7	13.3	14.8
34	6.1	12.5	1.1	2.7	2.3	20.2	13.3

Engineer	Farmer/ forester	Health prof.	Lawyer	Nurse	Research scientist	Other choice	Undecided
2.5	1.9	2.5	3.8	0.0	0.6	10.1	9.5
1.4	0.0	11.0	7.5	0.7	2.7	21.9	6.8
4.9	0.6	9.0	1.7	0.6	1.4	12.4	12.1
0.0	0.0	7.6	0.0	1.5	1.5	18.2	13.6
0.5	0.5	3.2	0.9	15.2	1.4	20.3	12.0
2.3	0.6	5.2	0.0	0.0	2.9	28.3	14.5
1.1	0.0	3.4	4.5	1.9	0.8	24.4	4.1
0.0	0.0	2.3	0.0	1.2	1.2	48.8	7.0
0.7	0.0	2.7	0.0	0.0	0.0	2.1	3.4
3.8	0.2	1.9	6.9	0.2	1.2	17.0	8.1
0.7	2.9	2.9	5.1	0.7	4.4	9.6	12.5
2.2	2.2	2.2	1.1	1.1	1.1	14.4	11.6
1.5	3.8	3.8	6.0	0.0	3.8	16.5	13.5
6.2	4.1	4.1	2.8	13.1	2.8	9.7	9.0
0.0	2.2	2.2	0.7	22.1	1.5	20.6	7.4
5.8	8.7	8.7	1.4	2.9	3.6	19.6	9.4
3.6	4.6	4.6	1.8	7.7	3.9	18.0	12.3
3.9	7.4	7.4	5.0	0.4	2.1	11.7	9.2
0.0	17.2	17.2	1.1	0.0	3.4	32.2	4.6
0.0	2.4	2.4	4.2	0.5	2.1	16.3	6.8
1.9	3.9	3.9	2.3	0.0	1.9	20.2	12.0
0.0	10.4	10.4	0.0	32.8	1.5	7.5	3.0
0.0	1.4	1.4	1.4	14.5	0.0	20.3	8.7
0.1	3.5	3.5	0.6	0.8	0.4	21.5	23.0
1.5	5.1	5.1	3.7	0.7	4.4	17.6	5.9
2.2	1.7	1.7	9.0	0.2	3.4	21.8	16.0
0.0	4.9	4.9	0.0	0.0	0.0	2.4	0.0
4.0	6.7	6.7	4.3	0.0	4.3	26.8	10.7
0.0	3.9	3.9	0.6	1.1	5.1	24.2	27.5
1.1	2.2	2.2	2.2	0.0	3.3	8.7	9.8
0.6	4.9	4.9	6.1	0.9	2.9	33.2	6.6
4.8	3.7	3.7	5.9	0.5	1.6	16.0	10.1
3.1	5.9	5.9	0.4	14.8	2.0	21.1	5.1
0.8	5.3	5.3	3.0	1.1	3.0	22.8	5.7

TABLE A-3 *(continued)*

Institution	Artist	Business-man	Clergy-man	College teacher	Doctor	Educator (secondary)	Elem. teacher
35	6.3	10.7	2.0	0.5	2.4	19.0	11.2
36	14.6	2.1	0.0	0.0	0.0	20.8	25.0
37	2.2	20.9	1.4	0.0	0.7	16.5	10.1
38	9.0	10.2	0.0	0.0	2.4	23.5	8.4
39	6.2	6.2	3.7	1.2	1.2	19.8	18.5
40	0.0	7.9	1.6	1.6	3.2	22.2	36.5

TABLE A-4 *Career plans of entering freshman classes at 23 elite colleges, 1969*

Institution	Artist	Business-man	Clergy-man	College teacher	Doctor	Educator (secondary)	Elem. teacher
01	1.0	0.5	0.0	5.1	1.0	0.5	0.0
02	0.0	1.9	0.1	4.6	0.0	0.9	0.0
03	5.9	3.4	0.5	2.4	10.2	13.7	4.9
04	9.9	1.0	0.5	1.5	2.8	15.1	5.0
05	8.6	2.1	0.5	1.6	5.9	9.6	3.7
06	11.6	3.6	0.6	4.8	7.4	8.3	2.7
07	4.8	5.1	0.3	2.0	7.6	19.8	2.5
08	5.3	12.2	0.4	6.1	13.8	6.9	0.0
09	8.7	5.3	0.8	0.8	6.8	11.7	1.9
10	8.7	6.2	1.0	6.2	10.0	4.5	0.3
11	9.6	0.6	0.0	2.9	5.4	8.6	3.3
12	3.7	7.7	0.0	3.1	16.1	3.7	0.0
13	5.1	2.6	0.3	6.6	8.6	9.1	0.6
14	2.4	12.0	0.5	3.7	14.3	5.0	0.0
15	15.6	1.9	0.0	2.6	6.7	8.2	2.4
16	0.0	0.0	0.0	0.0	0.0	0.0	0.0
17	12.4	1.6	1.2	6.6	7.0	7.9	2.3
18	13.3	1.4	0.4	8.4	3.9	4.9	1.4
19	5.4	1.9	1.3	2.7	10.4	7.1	1.5
20	4.2	4.2	0.6	7.9	15.2	7.3	0.0
21	8.0	1.6	1.0	5.8	8.3	7.7	1.0
22	39.9	0.6	0.0	0.6	1.7	3.5	1.7
23	9.3	6.3	0.5	3.0	4.8	13.1	0.8

Engineer	Farmer/ forester	Health prof.	Lawyer	Nurse	Research scientist	Other choice	Undecided
3.4	2.9	2.9	3.9	0.5	0.5	18.0	14.1
0.0	12.5	12.5	2.1	0.0	0.0	18.8	4.2
1.4	5.8	5.8	3.6	0.7	1.4	12.9	19.4
3.0	3.6	3.6	1.2	0.6	1.2	15.1	19.3
2.5	2.5	2.5	1.2	6.2	3.7	12.3	13.6
0.0	0.0	0.0	3.2	0.0	0.0	12.7	11.1

Engineer	Farmer/ forester	Health prof.	Lawyer	Nurse	Research scientist	Other choice	Undecided
17.9	1.0	0.0	0.5	0.0	55.6	4.1	12.8
35.2	0.0	0.0	0.9	0.0	37.0	6.5	13.0
2.9	0.5	3.4	9.8	0.0	5.9	19.5	17.1
0.0	0.3	1.5	3.3	1.0	3.3	32.9	23.1
0.0	0.0	1.1	6.4	0.0	3.7	39.0	17.6
0.6	0.9	1.8	5.7	0.6	5.4	19.6	26.5
2.0	1.1	1.4	7.6	0.0	7.1	18.4	20.1
5.3	0.4	0.8	20.3	0.0	5.3	8.1	15.0
2.7	0.8	1.5	5.3	0.0	4.2	29.5	20.1
1.4	0.0	0.7	14.9	0.0	14.2	7.6	24.2
0.2	0.6	2.1	3.5	0.8	6.7	25.9	29.9
2.8	0.9	0.6	16.4	0.0	6.8	11.5	26.6
1.7	0.9	0.6	6.6	0.0	6.0	15.7	35.7
8.1	0.7	0.3	17.2	0.0	6.7	9.4	19.7
0.0	0.5	2.2	5.5	0.2	5.0	29.3	19.7
72.7	0.0	0.0	0.0	0.0	0.0	27.3	0.0
1.4	0.4	0.4	4.8	0.0	6.4	17.4	30.2
1.8	1.1	0.4	2.5	0.0	9.1	16.8	34.7
1.0	0.0	1.3	24.4	0.4	5.0	20.2	17.5
0.6	0.6	1.2	13.9	0.0	6.7	10.3	27.3
4.8	0.3	0.3	7.4	0.0	9.6	17.0	27.2
0.0	0.0	1.2	1.2	0.0	0.6	17.9	31.2
1.3	1.3	1.8	5.8	0.0	6.3	22.2	23.5

Appendix B: The Inventory of College Activities Factors: Key to Figures 3 to 6

The Peer Environment

Interpersonal behavior

1 *Competitiveness versus cooperativeness* Students at institutions which score at the competitive end of this bipolar factor are inclined to take risks, to be impulsive and somewhat irresponsible, and to have an aggressive desire to win out over others. Students at institutions scoring at the cooperative pole participate more in group activities, have strong religious inclinations, and are sensitive to and concerned about the needs of others.

2 *Organized dating* This factor indicates the frequency of formal and prearranged dating at an institution; students at high-scoring institutions tend to have blind dates and to go to parties and dances.

3 *Independence* This factor correlates closely with verbal aggressiveness and, to a lesser extent, with rate of drinking. Students at high-scoring institutions tend to argue a lot with other students, to demonstrate against administrative policies, and to participate in sports. In addition, they are highly able academically and come from families who are well educated; they have high degree aspirations, they study a great deal, and they frequently plan careers as scientists or as entrepreneurs.

4 *Cohesiveness* Institutions scoring high on this dimension are characterized by warmth and friendliness. Students tend to come from rural backgrounds, to value getting along with others, and to have several close friends on campus. At low-scoring institutions, on the other hand, students are likely to come from urban backgrounds, to be highly able academically, to regard themselves as unconventional, and to place a high value on originality.

5 *Informal dating* At high-scoring institutions, students tend to have many dates of an informal or casual variety (coke, coffee, and study dates). They frequently report having fallen in love or having broken up with a boyfriend or girlfriend during the freshman year. At low-scoring institutions, students frequently complain about having too few dates.

Noninterpersonal behavior

6 *Femininity* Students at high-scoring institutions (often women's colleges) frequently engage in such "feminine" activities as trying on clothes in a store without buying anything, taking dietary formulas, attending ballet performances or fashion shows, crying, and talking over personal problems with friends. They tend to major in the arts or in social fields (elementary and secondary teaching, social welfare, nursing, etc.). Students at low-scoring institutions (often men's colleges) major in science and technology and spend more time gambling, playing chess, and participating in or discussing sports.

7 *Drinking versus religiousness* Institutions which rank at the high end of this bipolar factor are characterized by students who do a relatively large amount of social drinking. They also tend to argue with other students and with their instructors and to be independent and competitive. These students are usually above average in academic ability. Students at institutions which score at the opposite end of this factor rate themselves as very religious and tend to engage in such behaviors as attending church or Sunday School, saying grace before meals, praying, and reading the Bible. Their average academic ability is usually low.

8 *Musical and artistic activity* Students at these institutions manifest a strong interest in the arts. They frequently attend recitals, concerts, stage plays, and exhibits. In addition, they are inclined to be musicians or artists themselves; to participate in informal group singing and in more formal musical, dramatic, and artistic activities; and to major in artistic fields.

9 *Leisure time* Students at high-scoring institutions spend a relatively large amount of time going to movies and plays and playing games. They value having a good time and getting along with other people.

10 *Career indecision* Students at high-scoring institutions are inclined to change both their major fields and their career plans;

frequently, they are clients of the counseling center at their institution.

11 *Regularity of sleeping habits* Students at high-scoring institutions tend to get a great deal of sleep. Frequently, they live at home, are Roman Catholic, rate themselves as highly religious, and attend church regularly. Students at low-scoring institutions tend to stay up all night, to take pills to stay awake, to nap during the day, and to oversleep and miss classes. They usually live on campus during the freshman year, and many of them come from a high socioeconomic Protestant background.

12 *Use of library* Students at high-scoring institutions frequently study in the library and check out a relatively large number of books and journals. They read for pleasure a good deal, and they tend to feel that college should provide a basic education and appreciation of ideas.

13 *Conflict with regulations* Institutions where students frequently lose privileges because of infractions of college regulations tend to be Roman Catholic rather than Protestant or nonsectarian. The students themselves engage in such religious activities as attending church and praying.

14 *Student employment* At institutions scoring high on this factor, a relatively large proportion of the students work for pay during the school year. They spend comparatively little time studying, and frequently they cheat on examinations.

15 *Use of automobiles* This factor is defined by the proportion of students who drive cars during the school year. Predominantly black colleges tend to score low.

The Classroom Environment

16 *Involvement in the class* At high-scoring institutions, both students and instructors tend to show an interest in the class. The instructor (who is likely to be a woman) encourages discussion, knows students by their first names, takes attendance regularly, and often gives "pop" quizzes. The students are likely to major in education and social science. At institutions scoring low on this factor, classes tend to be large. The instructors are frequently involved in research. The students are highly able academically, and a high proportion major in the sciences. They rarely speak out in class unless called upon, and they often oversleep and miss class.

17 *Verbal aggressiveness* This factor covers such classroom behaviors as arguing with the instructor and with other students, asking questions freely, and making wisecracks. At high-scoring institutions, examinations are usually of the "essay" type rather than "objective." Students tend to be independent, to work on the campus newspaper or be varsity athletes, to come from a suburban area, and to plan on doing graduate work.

18 *Extraversion of the instructor* At high-scoring institutions, students tend to report that the instructor is enthusiastic, has a good sense of humor, and is well-grounded in the subject matter. At low-scoring institutions, instructors are frequently regarded as dull and uninteresting and as tending to speak in a monotone.

19 *Familiarity with the instructor* Students at high-scoring institutions frequently report that they know the instructor's first name and that they were guests at the instructor's house or saw the instructor in his office. High-scoring institutions tend to be small and residential.

20 *Organization in the classroom* This factor involves the degree of structuring in the class. At high-scoring institutions, instructors take attendance and assign seats. Classes meet at regularly scheduled times and places, and students tend to be on time to class.

21 *Severity of grading* This dimension is defined by the proportion of students who receive at least one failing grade during the freshman year. At high-scoring institutions, students receive relatively poor grades; they rarely type their written assignments. In addition, they have relatively low academic ability, come from a rather poor socioeconomic background, and feel that the chief value of college is to provide career training. At low-scoring institutions, students tend to be academically able and interested in the arts and literature.

The Administrative Environment

22 *Severity of administrative policy against drinking* High-scoring institutions, which are often sectarian, have relatively harsh policies against student drinking. Students at these colleges tend to rate themselves as highly religious and to engage in religious activities. At low-scoring institutions, which are usually private and nonsectarian, students do a fair amount of drinking. They are highly able academically and frequently plan to get the Ph.D. The classroom environments at low-scoring institutions are permis-

sive, and the college has the image of being liberal and granting the student a good deal of independence.

23 *Severity of administrative policy against aggression*   Students at high-scoring institutions are penalized fairly heavily for such behaviors as demonstrating against an administrative policy, having water fights, and raiding dormitories. Students are more apt to report that student publications are censored and that their fellow students are conformists. At low-scoring institutions, students are highly able academically, come from high socioeconomic backgrounds, and feel that the intellectual environment is theoretical rather than practical and that their fellow students are of very high intellectual caliber.

24 *Severity of administrative policy against heterosexual activity*   High-scoring colleges have strict regulations against a student's being alone with a date in a dormitory room and coming in late to class. (These regulations tend to be applied more strictly to women.) Students at these colleges rate themselves as religious and engage in religious activities; they feel that censorship is imposed on student publications and that the environment can be classified as Victorian. Students at low-scoring institutions are more able academically, regard the college as liberal, and feel that they are given considerable independence.

25 *Severity of administrative policy against cheating*   High-scoring institutions typically expel students who are found cheating on examinations. The rate of cheating, as reported by the students themselves, tends to be low.

The College Image

26 *Academic competitiveness*   Students at high-scoring institutions—who usually are superior academically, come from a high socioeconomic background, and plan to major in a scientific field and to get the Ph.D.—feel that the atmosphere is competitive, that their fellow students are of exceptional academic caliber, that they themselves are under pressure to get good grades, and that their college is superior to other colleges and has an outstanding national reputation. Students at low-scoring institutions report that intellectual activity is limited, that not enough work is required of them, and that the atmosphere is carefree.

27 *Concern for the individual student*   Students at high-scoring institutions feel that faculty and upperclassmen go out of their way

to be helpful; they rate the environment as warm, friendly, and high in morale. Interpersonal relationships tend to be cooperative rather than competitive, and students spend a good deal of time participating in or attending musical, dramatic, and artistic activities. Students at low-scoring institutions report that they felt lost when they first came to campus and that students are treated "like numbers in a book." They say that they do not have enough personal contact with their instructors, who seem to be more interested in research than in teaching, and they feel that the campus is too big.

28 *School spirit* Students at high-scoring institutions see the environments as high in morale and as fostering poise and maturity. They express overall satisfaction with college. Students at low-scoring institutions, who often come from urban backgrounds and live at home during the freshman year, feel that the other students are apathetic and not well-rounded. They say that there is little to do on campus but to attend class and to study.

29 *Permissiveness* This factor is associated with ratings of the college as "liberal" and with students' impressions that they are granted considerable independence, that instructors are lenient in interpreting regulations, and that the intellectual atmosphere is theoretical rather than practical. In addition, at high-scoring institutions, classes are run in an informal manner, and students say that many of their fellows are avant-garde and care little about personal appearance. Relatively frequent drinking is also characteristic of these colleges. At institutions scoring low on this factor, students rate themselves as religious and engage in religious activities. They see the college environment as Victorian, and they feel that student publications are censored by the administration and that a narrow political point of view dominates the campus. Administrative policies against drinking, aggression, and heterosexual behavior are severe.

30 *Snobbishness* Students at high-scoring institutions rate the atmosphere as snobbish and sophisticated and report that they frequently felt out of place on the campus and that the proportion of avant-garde students on campus is relatively large. They tend to come from a fairly high socioeconomic background and to attend foreign films. Students at low-scoring institutions rate the environment as practical-minded and realistic.

31 *Emphasis on athletics* Students at high-scoring institutions feel that athletics are overemphasized, that athletes are given special privileges, and that there is little to do at the college except go to class and study. They spend a proportionately large amount of time watching sports events. Students at low-scoring institutions complain that they do not get enough exercise.

32 *Flexibility of the curriculum* Low-scoring institutions are viewed by their students as requiring too much course work. In addition, students complain that they do not have enough freedom in selecting courses, that they are not given enough time for extracurricular activities, and that there are too few outlets for creative activities.

33 *Emphasis on social life* Students at high-scoring institutions characterize the atmosphere as social and carefree. They say also that too much emphasis is given to social activities, that it is important to belong to the right clubs, that fraternities and sororities are too dominant, that their fellow students are conforming, and that intellectual activity on the campus is low. Students at low-scoring institutions say that they do not have enough dates or enough time for social activity and that there is little to do on campus except go to class and study.

Appendix C: Administrators' Views of the Problems Facing Their Colleges

The following are written comments received from various administrators at some of the invisible colleges in our sample. They were responding to the question: "What do you regard as the major problems confronting your college?" Interspersed with the comments are the first-hand observations that one of the authors made of two of the institutions.

A COEDUCA-
TIONAL
LUTHERAN
COLLEGE IN
ILLINOIS

Comments of the vice-president for finance

1 Finances (natch!). We are trying to do some of the things that we feel should have been done long ago in our area. A present current surplus accumulated over the years supports this effort but is running out. Supposedly, the tuition and fee costs necessary to support this program tend to eliminate the kind of a regional student we should speak to because neither he nor we have sufficient funds to pay the cost. We want to avoid becoming an "elite" college.

2 Regional effort. The Indian people and rural (church member?) people live in our area. We have a very difficult time finding Indians to come to our college, even with subsistence. What can be done to create a desire on the part of the tribe to encourage education other than vocationally oriented? We feel the morals of our generation and the preceding generation still have value—and increasing value—today. We would like to preserve these values, even though the trend is against it. We "battle" our students on this issue.

Comments of the president

1 Financial support adequate for us to perform our function as a private church-related college is a concern. However, even more

important for our future is the relationship of our college to our church, our service region, and our image.

2   The relationship of our college to our church. We need to face such questions as: Do we (the college) need the church? Does the church need us? How can we best serve our church? Do we lead the church or follow their direction? What is distinctive, or should be, about a "Christian college"?

3   The relationship of our college to our service region. What are our responsibilities to our population-declining agricultural region? Are such ventures as we now are promoting (a Center for Community Organization and Area Development and a Continuing Education Program) appropriate?

4   How can we change our image? Is a national reputation necessary for survival? Should we more actively "toot our own horn"?

A COEDUCA-TIONAL METHODIST COLLEGE IN IOWA

Comments of a faculty member

1   Development of an organizational plan. Basically, our loose organization is excessively expensive and educationally inefficient, and it creates a moral problem. Freedoms and excesses practiced by administrative officers should be curbed. Job descriptions and authority of minor "offices" should be clearly stated.

2   The ability to select and maintain a purpose and type of institution. Because of administrative mobility, lack of money, and lack of organization and structure, the small college drifts according to the pressures applied. These pressures may be in the form of new administrative officers, changes in governing boards, little power struggles within the college, and donors.

Comments of the graduate school director

1   We have too many colleges and universities in our area. Our state is decreasing in population, but new colleges are being added and talked about. There should be some large planning group to regulate the formation and location of new colleges. We have also been hurt by a state network of vocational schools and junior colleges. There are simply not enough students to fill all the institutions in our area.

Comments of the academic dean

1 Keeping the institution in the mainstream of higher education in America

2 Recruiting topflight faculty members and holding them

3 Bringing in outstanding people to inspire and motivate the faculty and the students

4 Providing in-service training for trustees

5 Involving the college in problems of the local community, area, and region

6 Acquiring technical staff to help put together outstanding proposals for foundations and the U.S. government

7 Keeping the institution from attempting too many programs and projects which we can't do well

8 Staying on the track of doing well a few things rather than copying the big state universities

Comments of the president

As our college faces the future, I think we must concentrate upon what we can do best: the liberal arts program. I think that we should strive for excellence in all aspects. That is our hope, our salvation, our justification for being. When I speak of excellence I am thinking of excellence in *ideals, alertness* to the changes which the times thrust upon us, and *identifying* with the region we serve. Excellence will require our breaking away from our "provincialism" and broadening our understanding of other cultures.

Observations of author

I saw many signs of affluence on the campus: new buildings, well-dressed students, and new equipment and facilities.

People tended to be excessively polite. I kept wondering, is it the South, the strong sectarian affiliation, or what? The politeness makes one uncomfortable at first, but then you come to respect it and to be more considered and reserved in your own remarks.

People were temperate and restrained. I think that they just remained silent on those matters where my ideas were so far out that they saw no possibility of constructive dialogue or reconciliation.

The *in loco parentis* doctrine is just about as severely applied here as is possible these days: no drinking or dancing. Until recently, smoking was completely forbidden, but now it is permitted in the dorms but not in the classes. Some students I talked to said that at least half of the students drink regularly (estimates ran as high as 80 percent) and that the regulations are poorly enforced.

There seems to be a peculiar discrepancy between the perceptions of the president and the realities of student conduct. When I asked him in the morning if some of the students were hippie types, he said that a few students last year had tried to grow long hair and wear beads, but that they had "managed to talk most of them out of it." That same afternoon, I talked to a student who had a beard and asked him if any pressure had been put on him to get rid of it. He said no, and appeared somewhat surprised that I had even asked him. The president and some of his staff were also inclined to dismiss the amount of student drinking as involving "only a small minority." This lack of awareness on the part of the administration could lead to very serious problems, it seems to me.

The president seems to feel that relaxing the *in loco parentis* policy will alienate the "constituency."

A COED PRESBYTERIAN COLLEGE IN WEST VIRGINIA

Comments of a development officer

During the past 15 years we have moved rapidly up the "quality" scale, at least in the context of this state. At the same time, presumably with some cause-effect relationship, our in-state enrollment has dropped from 50 percent to 16 percent. The board and administration want more area students and want to do or become whatever is necessary to reach them. Most of the faculty want bright students, and the local region be hanged!

To maintain the relatively high standards we have achieved, *and* to serve our area, will require, among other things, fantastic sums of money!

We have 850 students and probably must have about 1,200 to keep alive in the long haul.

Comments of the dean of the faculty

The gravest problem faced by this college is financial. It lacks endowment. Its tuition and fees are very high, thus it has "priced itself out of the market" so far as regional students are concerned. It now has, but is slowly losing, an excellent faculty. Unless the financial problems are solved, there is not much hope for the future. Tax-supported institutions can do the job of providing various types of academic and vocational training. What is needed, and what this institution could and should provide, is broad liberal education of high quality in an area that needs to have at least one college committed to "raising the sights" of the people, rather than merely "taking them where they are," merely attracting students who can and will go to a mediocre program anyway. The great need is to serve those who desire and would profit from a liberal education, but who, in fact, will probably never enter any sort of college.

**A PREDOMI-
NANTLY
BLACK
COLLEGE IN
TENNESSEE**

Comments of the president

What this institution needs is:

1   More communication between departments, a flow of data from the top downward

2   Money for in-service training for student personnel staff

3   Special programs for the slow student (tutoring)

4   Money to bring speakers to the campus and to sponsor more cultural activities

The future roles, as I perceive them, for this college are:

1   The training of college teachers in new kinds of philosophies which will give new educational directions to programs for a variety of human abilities

2   The development of aggressive recruitment efforts to make possible opportunities for other people to acquire college experiences (classical and/or nonclassical)

3   The development of realistic and substantive programs in community service which are central to the educational objectives of the college (black colleges must exert substantive efforts to upgrade black people in black communities)

Observations of author

I was surprised by the contemporary look of many of the students: afros and sunglasses displayed by several (men much more than women), many beards and sideburns worn, and hippie-type clothing worn by a few men (vests, granny glasses, and blue-denim work clothes).

Students in the class I spoke to barely said a word. They looked either bored or suspicious, I couldn't tell which. Maybe neither—possibly they were just sizing me up. But the blank expressions were a little disconcerting.

An administrator said that over $3,000 per student was spent for educational and general purposes. I find this difficult to believe. Is this correct? Is it true for other invisible colleges?

Less than 90 percent of the students live on campus. They have just finished a shiny new dormitory which will hold more than 600 students. I was appalled at the mess in the men's room (filthy sinks, dirty paper towels all over the floor) and in the cafeteria, at the place where trays are turned in (trays with dirty dishes all over the floor, many dishes broken, food all over the place). Apparently, the trays were being returned to the window faster than the kitchen help could take them in, so the students were stacking them up so high that some of them were sliding off the pile and crashing on the floor. No one, apparently, had even tried to pick up the mess; they just walked away and left it. I am trying to figure out if this is circumstantial—the new bathrooms and cafeteria are still not debugged—or whether this unconcern over messiness is characteristic of the students.

Fraternity and sorority hazing is practiced. What I could see was very strange: students in groups of five or six, all dressed alike, walking—no, *marching*—in single file, almost in lockstep. All the time, everywhere they marched. I was told that this goes on for *a month* prior to initiation and that the initiations still involve a lot of brutal and humiliating ordeals, including beatings. Another strange, almost anachronistic, aspect of the system is that it was begun only 15 years ago and that it has slowly been gaining strength. Still, only a minority of students join. I was told that there is no rivalry between the fraternity members and the independents but that the rivalry among the different fraternities and sororities is intense. Recruiting of pledges is active and vigorous. When I asked why freshmen would want to join—with the hazing and brutality—my host reflected for a moment, and then said that it must give the student a feeling of status or of belonging. The apparent indifference to this of the faculty and administrators with whom I talked was puzzling.

The faculty has adopted a new curriculum involving interdisciplinary courses, with five-week "modules" in social service, natural science, and humanities, as well as an orientation course at the beginning. Faculty teach these in teams, sitting in on each other's sessions and sometimes participating. At my urging, they have set up an experiment in which every fifth or sixth freshman in 1969 is taking the old standard curriculum, and the rest are enrolled in the new curriculum. The same teachers teach in both programs. They administered a battery of "placement" tests when the students started, and I have urged them to retest the students after one or two years. I was so impressed by their bringing off their experiment so well that I offered to help them analyze their data when they finish the retesting.

A COEDUCA-TIONAL METHODIST COLLEGE IN KENTUCKY

Comments of the business manager-treasurer

1   Retaining students. Our loss over the four-year period is entirely too high.

2   Strengthening recruiting policies. How to do this is a matter of uncertainty at the present, but we feel there is a relationship between this problem and the matter of retention of students through the four-year period of their education.

A COEDUCA-TIONAL LUTHERAN COLLEGE IN NEBRASKA

Comments of the business manager

Administrators may not be really capable of doing what they *should be doing* and the personnel isn't deep enough to bring up complementary ability from the ranks. Perhaps the selection of personnel who will actually do what they know should be done is the key.

"Leadership" as the one biggest problem is perhaps an oversimplification of "problems."

A COEDUCA-TIONAL LUTHERAN COLLEGE IN NEBRASKA

Comments of the dean

1   Financial problems. Sixty to seventy percent of the funds come from tuition and fees. Increased costs of operation make it necessary to keep increasing tuition and fees. The competition of state colleges with low tuition and fees makes it *difficult to draw* students. Reduced financial support from the church.

2   The above limits other aspects of the college: equipment, faculty salaries, scholarships, etc.

A ROMAN CATHOLIC WOMEN'S COLLEGE IN NEBRASKA

Comments of the president

1   Organization. Attracting top-notch administrators to a small institution and not having top people wear "too many hats" in the institution who are therefore unable to function effectively at their main job. This implies inadequate staffing, which goes back to the financial aspect.

2   Recruitment of students. Several problems arise in this area: The college is small, church-related, and all-women — concepts which are not too "popular" at the present time. Competition with other institutions that offer more "attractions," but not necessarily a better education, seems almost to force the smaller institution to focus on things of lesser significance.

A COEDUCA-TIONAL PRESBYTERIAN COLLEGE IN NORTH DAKOTA

Comments of the president

1   Economic pressures. The same forces mentioned above suggest some unattractive alternatives, such as (a) offering less than competitive faculty salaries to keep the cost down, (b) increasing tuition to levels unattractive to in-state students, (c) using up endowment to meet operating costs, and (d) increasing faculty-student ratios. We have decided we must charge students more, continue to invest more in faculty, and sacrifice at the point of the faculty-student ratio.

A COEDUCA-TIONAL NONSEC-TARIAN COLLEGE IN KENTUCKY

Comments of the president

1   One of our major problems is getting more students. At present, this need is more important than getting more financial support. To get more students, we need to do two things: (a) do a better job of selling our present program and (b) develop a better program.

2   Financial support is another major problem and is necessary to meet the objectives stated above.

Index